Experiencing Nature With Young Children:
Awakening Delight, Curiosity, and a Sense of Stewardship

Alice Sterling Honig

Experiencing Nature With Young Children

Awakening Delight, Curiosity, and a Sense of Stewardship

Alice Sterling Honig

National Association for the Education of Young Children
Washington DC

National Association for the
Education of Young Children
1313 L Street NW, Suite 500
Washington, DC 20005-4101
202-232-8777 • 800-424-2460
www.naeyc.org

NAEYC Books

Chief Publishing Officer, *Derry Koralek*

Editor-in-Chief, *Kathy Charner*

Director of Creative Services,
Edwin C. Malstrom

Managing Editor, *Mary Jaffe*

Senior Editor, *Holly Bohart*

Senior Graphic Designer,
Malini Dominey

Associate Editor, *Elizabeth Wegner*

Editorial Assistant, *Ryan Smith*

Permissions

Excerpt on pages 58–59 is reprinted, by permission, from K. Constantine, "Reflection: Earth Agent Day Adventures," *Wonder: Newsletter of the Nature Action Collaborative for Children* (January/February 2013): 96. Copyright © Exchange Press, Inc. All rights reserved.

Excerpt on page 59 is reprinted, by permission, from N. Rosenow, "Children Are 'Speaking' to Us Through Their Construction Work: Are We 'Listening?,'" *Exchange* 199 (May/June 2011): 63. Copyright © Exchange Press, Inc. All rights reserved.

Photo Credits

Cover photograph copyright © Shutterstock

Copyright © Rebecca Anlas: 17, 30 (bottom), 58; Toby Armstrong/© NAEYC: 45 (bottom); Natalie Bennett: 54 (top); Bonnie Blagojevic: 18 (bottom), 35; Carly Brown: 40; Hayley Burns: 5, 15 (top); Frances Carlson: 56 (bottom); Matt Cormons: 14, 21, 23, 38, 43, 44, 45 (top), 46 (bottom), 53, 68, 70, 71; Malini Dominey: viii, 60, 61 (leaf), 64; Cynthia Duke: 57; Mary Duru: 18 (top), 49; Susanna Feder: 20, 55 (top); Sandra Lighter-Jones: 62 (bottom); Julia Luckenbill: 2, 7 (bottom), 8, 9, 15 (bottom), 22, 24, 48, 55 (bottom), 63; Beth Ann Moore: 54 (bottom); NAEYC: 46 (top), 50, 51; New Canaan Nature Center: 73; Elisabeth Nichols: 19 (bottom), 29, 31 (top); Marilyn Nolt: 11; Karen Phillips: 3, 10, 12, 19 (top), 28, 30 (top), 33 (bottom), 36, 37 (top), 56 (top); Deborah Pruitt: 6; Jude Keith Rose: 1, 13, 31 (bottom), 32 (bottom), 33 (top), 39, 41; Michael Rosen: 47; Ellen B. Senisi: 25, 37 (bottom), 62 (top), 66; Courtney Shivetts: 27; Kathy Sible: 32 (top); Thinkstock: 1 (bird), 4, 5 (pinecone), 7 (top), 16, 17 (squirrel), 26, 27 (ladybug), 34, 35 (butterfly), 42, 43 (frog), 52, 53 (fern), 61, 65 (sunflower), 65, 69, 74, 75 (mushroom); Susan Woog Wagner/© NAEYC: 72

Courtesy of the author: 67

Credits

Cover design: Edwin C. Malstrom

Proofreader: Heather Collick

Library of Congress Control Number: 2014948351

ISBN: 978-1-938113-07-9

Item 1128

Contents

Introduction

A child's early passion for caring about nature and the environment can be the catalyst for a lifelong commitment to conserve the earth's resources. The last decade has witnessed a growing interest in and concern about children's connection to nature. So that they can one day contribute solutions to the challenges of global climate changes, children need to experience the pleasures of outdoors (World Forum Foundation & Community Playthings 2013) and develop a sense of awe and appreciation of nature. A deeply felt joy in the wonders of nature arises as children watch autumn leaves flare into a glory of colors or see a brilliant rainbow arching the whole sky after a drenching rain. Even an infant lying on a blanket in the grass swivels to look at amazing sights in every direction—grass, flowers, tiny insects. Adults need to begin early to awaken and heighten children's awareness of the fragility of nature and of humans' responsibilities for keeping it a safe and enjoyable place for all.

Teachers of young children have a great deal of responsibility. They help children learn how to share and care for others, develop empathy and make friends with peers, develop their thinking and problem-solving skills, and master difficult emotions with self-control. Teachers also support children's emergent literacy, science and math skills, creative skills, and health and motor development through vigorous play. The challenge, then, is how to embed a passion for nature learning and conservation into other areas of the curriculum.

When children play outdoors, they rejoice in using their muscles to chase, climb, jump, and run freely in space, and this activity builds active, healthy bodies. Yet much high-level thinking also occurs outdoors; children solve problems, negotiate game rules, and construct huts or build a snowman. In forest kindergartens, children are often outside a large part of the day for their learning experiences. Both indoor and outdoor nature activities help integrate their understanding and enthusiasm for helping the earth (Nature Explore 2011). Some schools use gardening to enhance nature appreciation and enjoyment; gardening also develops children's skills in academic areas. In Yuma, Arizona, children planted and cared for vegetables in raised gardens; in just one year, the school's fourth-grade science scores increased 17 percent (Buczynski 2013). Students brought most of the produce home for their families, but after the June harvest they donated almost 700 pounds of vegetables, including zucchini, green beans, tomatoes, watermelons, and honeydew melons, to the Yuma Community Food Bank.

Such experiences underscore the wide-ranging effects of early nature experiences.

Teachers are children's personal guides to awaken a sense of awe and rejoicing in the variety and richness of nature (Rivkin 2014) and deepen a desire to become creative conservers of the environment. Integrating nature learning into children's everyday experiences is a wonderful vehicle for sparking children's learning in all areas. The ideas in *Experiencing Nature With Young Children: Awakening Delight, Curiosity, and a Sense of Stewardship* will help children learn from and through nature.

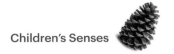

1 Awaken Children's Senses to Delight in Nature

Infants' and young children's earliest learning is through their senses (Piaget 1952). At snack time, a toddler squeezes a hunk of banana luxuriously through her fingers; the slippery texture feels so interesting. Nestled in the arms of a caregiver who has carried him outdoors, a baby will even lean down and lick her salty arm! Walking in the vegetable garden with Dad, a young preschooler stops to pick a ripe red pepper from a plant and looks surprised as she adventurously bites and chews, experiencing this new taste. Helping young children tune in to safe sensory experiences that will further their learning as well as expand their interests and enjoyment is a desirable curriculum goal.

Smelling and Tasting

The senses of smell and taste are easy to awaken through nature. In a class garden children can grow sweet-smelling herbs, such as basil and oregano, to put into spaghetti dishes they help make. Jasmine plants grow sweet-scented flowers; juniper bushes grow berries that smell sharp and fresh when pressed open. Treat children to fragrances indoors, too—hyacinth and paperwhite narcissus bulbs flourish in a bowl with pebbles and water. (Be aware of children who may be allergic or sensitive to fragrances.) Slow-motion videos allow children to watch the buds of amaryllis, lilies, irises,

and other beauties unfolding into glowing, colorful flowers (for example, see Vorobyoff Productions at vimeo.com). After children notice the splendor of a drift of buttery yellow daffodils, read aloud Wordsworth's poem "I Wandered Lonely as a Cloud," which expresses the poet's deep delight after viewing dancing daffodils along a lakeshore. Breathtaking beauty in nature, whether a single flower growing between a crack in the sidewalk or an entire field of flowers, provides an intimate entry for children to resonate to the rhythms and cadences of poetry.

Meals and snack times provide daily opportunities to taste fresh vegetables and fruits and to arouse children's curiosity about their origins. Where do these foods come from? How do they grow? New words embellish tasting times as children crunch baby carrots, munch on strips of sweet red pepper, tickle the palate with a squirt of tangy lemon or sweet orange juice, and relish the sharp, zippy flavor of a slice of red radish. What are these foods called in the children's home languages? What other fruits and vegetables do they commonly eat at home?

Outdoors, children in boots and raincoats lift their faces to taste raindrops. With ecstatic glee a toddler, enjoying a warm rain, stretches his arms and fingers forward to catch the raindrops. Giving words to new sensory experiences expands children's vocabulary (Honig 2001).

Listening

In autumn in the north, listen for the distinct calls of wild geese flying in a V shape high in the sky as they head south for the winter. Awaken children's wonder for birds and their songs (Alderfer 2013). From a telephone wire or tree branch, a bird sings the same song over and over. Children can share birdcalls they may have heard near water, perhaps while on vacations with their families, such as the wild cry of seagulls or the mournful cry of loons. Can the children tell you that a crow must have hopped onto a tree branch outside the open classroom window when they hear the raucous *caw* of that intelligent bird? Share how crows drop hard nuts on a roadway so that cars passing by will crush the hard shells; the crows then hop down quickly and snatch up the nut meats. Clever!

As you show pictures of different birds, children may be intrigued to learn that there are talking birds, including mynah birds, parrots, and some cockatoos. Play a recording of bird songs to help children distinguish the chirping of a sparrow, a warbler's tunes, the imitative songs of a mockingbird, the low cooing sounds of a mourning dove, and the *meow* sounds of a catbird. Pictures of the birds help children identify the birds on the recording.

Listening to nature includes hearing weather sounds, such as the star-tling sounds of icy hailstones bouncing on a windowpane. During storms, listen with children for the whining sounds of strong winds whirling down the street. A sudden downpour sends raindrops drumming a thick *pitter-pat-ter* sound on the windows. Support older children's listening skills by asking, "How is this sound the *same* or *different* from the soft hissing of snow against a windowpane?" Understanding concepts such as same and different or opposites (such as loud vs. soft; bumpy vs. smooth; sweet vs. sour; wet vs. dry) is impor-tant for many areas of learning (Honig 1982). Discrimination skills are particu-larly important for emergent literacy, as young children learn to listen for *rhymes*, or words whose endings sound the same. Preschoolers delight in shouting out simple rhyming words such as *cat, bat, sat, fat, hat,* and so forth. In *Jam-berry* (Bruce Degen), a young boy and a friendly rhyme-spouting bear joyously romp through a fantasy berry world, and their outdoor adventures include rhyming chants such as "One berry, two berry, pick me a blueberry."

Seeing

Young children learn to discriminate visually between circles, squares, triangles, and other shapes. They can also recognize the shapes of living creatures. Identifying bird silhouettes or spying early spring flowers will

sharpen children's visual processing skills. Colorful pictures make it easier for children to triumphantly name each bird or plant they are learning to recognize.

What's that weed? Play I Spy with weeds. Take a weed walk around your setting and help children sharpen their observation and labeling skills as they hunt for and recognize Queen Anne's lace, dandelions, Veronica, thistles, Asian day flowers, lady's thumb (each leaf bears an inky "thumbprint"), wild daisies, chickweed, butter-and-eggs with tiny yellow flowers, or any weed that grows in your area. Pokeweed grows tall, and its berries turn from bright green to glistening jet black over the long summer weeks. *Note: All mature parts of the pokeweed are poisonous.* Other weeds to search for are Virginia

creeper, blue cornflower, creeping Charlie, yellow hawkweed, tall mullein with yellow flowers, ragweed (which contributes to some children's misery from allergies), goldenrod, and bearded willow-herb (with tiny pink flowers at the top). What a satisfying feeling when a child identifies wild-growing plants!

Showing the children photos of weeds and bringing the photos on a weed walk makes it easier to spot curbside weeds. Create a classroom bulletin board where children check off those they have proudly discovered already: Attach a photo of a plant discovery next to the child discoverer's name and photo, and children can share how they came to notice that plant.

With any plant, teach children to be safe. In addition to pokeweed, some of the other weeds discussed here, including Queen Anne's lace and

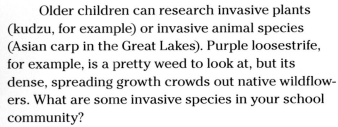

Virginia creeper, are poisonous. Other types of trees, bushes, and flowers are also toxic, including some of the wildflowers discussed in the next section. Children should never eat any part of a plant growing outdoors or of houseplants, and they should touch them only if an adult says it is safe. You can find a list of common poisonous plants at http://aggie-horticulture.tamu.edu/earthkind/landscape/poisonous-plants-resources/common-poisonous-plants-and-plant-parts/. Familiarize yourself with the plants in your area and identify which ones are toxic.

Older children can research invasive plants (kudzu, for example) or invasive animal species (Asian carp in the Great Lakes). Purple loosestrife, for example, is a pretty weed to look at, but its dense, spreading growth crowds out native wildflowers. What are some invasive species in your school community?

Awaken an interest in wildflowers. During a park visit, look for endangered and federally or state-protected springtime wildflowers that children can teach others to cherish and preserve, such as trillium, trout lilies, jack-in-the-pulpit, mayapples, saxifrage, wild ginger, desert lupine, and brittlebush. Some wildflowers have surprising names that children may find humorous. Search for Dutchman's britches, lady slippers, Herb Robert with its dainty pink flowers, bunchberries, false Solomon Seal, climbing twining morning glory, and dainty meadow rue. Ask dual language learners for the names of flowers in their home language. If they aren't sure, find out together. Hydrophytes are plants that need lots of water. Xerophytes, such as cactus, can flour-

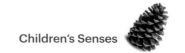

ish in dry environments. Can children find examples of both during the park visit or a neighborhood walk? Post photos of both types of plants in the classroom. Talk with the children about the similarities and differences between the two types of plants. Notice when they show sharp observation skills and can clearly describe what they have spied.

Just as there are rules for respecting other people and property, such as "Walk in the hallway," there are rules for caring for nature. Help children understand that picking flowers like tulips or daffodils diminishes their beauty because the flowers cannot grow back in the same year. But some plants, like clematis, snapdragons, roses, or red spirea, will indeed

bloom several times each season after their blooms are removed.

Compare the way materials look in shadow and in sunlight. Children are amazed to see how their shadows on the ground lengthen and shorten as the sun changes position. Even colors look different in bright, early morning sunshine than in the late afternoon light. Ask children to look at different natural materials they have collected, or they can experiment. On an outdoor picnic, for example, look at a sandwich first in sunlight and then in a shady spot. What do the children notice is different when full sunlight shines on an object? On a warm, sunny day, provide a hose and ask the children to stand with the sun at their backs and spray water carefully upward into the

Natural Defenses

Intrigued by the experience of different sensations when they explore the textures of natural materials, older children may ask why roses have such sharp thorns. This is a good opportunity to investigate some of the curious and interesting defenses that plants as well as animals have developed. Some defenses are *physical,* as when raspberry plants grow sharp prickles. Some plants use thorns for protection against munching critters. Children can experience thorns by growing lemon pits in soil in pots on a windowsill. As the plants grow, have children carefully feel the pointy lemon plant thorns, then rub their hands on the leaves and sniff

the citrus scent on their fingers. Some plants grow armor, as do porcupines and echidnas and some other spiny animals. Thus, coconut trees and other palms protect their fruit by physically growing many thick layers of coarse fibers around the trunk. In contrast, the leaves of holly plants are very smooth and slippery, making it difficult for bugs to feed on the leaves.

Some defenses are *chemical,* such as a sticky sap that some trees produce to trap bugs after some leaves have been damaged. If you have a piece of amber with a bug trapped inside, children can see how an ancient tree dripped sap down its trunk and trapped that now fossilized insect. Some bushes grow barbed leaves with poisons to deter goats and others from stripping their leaves. Geranium plants produce a unique chemical compound that lasts only a few hours; voracious Japanese beetles become disoriented from the chemical and may be consumed by predators during that short time, sparing the geranium.

Some animals, such as deer and antelope, run very fast to get away from a predator. Plants cannot run away, of course; they are rooted in soil. But some, like the sensitive mimosa, can quickly and tightly close their leaves when touched by an herbivore (a creature who eats vegetation), and this motion can also dislodge an insect bent on munching its leaves. In order to protect themselves, some plants live in friendly, helpful arrangements with other organisms. Fungi live on tall fescue plants, and the fungi produce toxins harmful to creatures that would attack the fescue. The plant and the fungi have a mutually helpful, or symbiotic, relationship.

tree leaves. They will laugh joyously when they see the beautiful rainbows that the sunlight and water create.

Gaze at clouds. Outdoor experiences do not always involve large muscle play. Nature provides rich opportunities that encompass imaginative viewing experiences, too. Lying on their backs in the grass, children gaze up at drifting clouds. Share the names for different kinds of clouds, such as *cirrus* or *cumulus*. Dreamily, each child imagines a particular, puffy cumulus cloud to be a grazing sheep, a dragon, a diving whale, or a boat sailing on the blue sea of the sky above. Imagination flows freely, and the visual scenes and imagined figures change slowly as clouds drift by. Encourage children to describe what they see. They might try to get others to

see the same thing by explaining what it is about the cloud formation that inspires their unique, personal view of that cloud. Children may want to draw their cloud-creation scenarios or even make up a poem about a scene they see pictured or sculpted in the clouds.

Watching clouds and identifying what they look like can boost children's understanding of metaphors and similes. A cloud *looks like* a whale or a puppy or a boat to a child. A teacher might look at a photo of a child's beloved new kitty and announces that the kitty is "as cute as a button." A pink-cheeked, curled-up-asleep baby is "a delicious little rosebud," exclaims the loving caregiver. Understanding such comparisons takes time and experience. I once visited a child care center and, seeing a darling toddler coming toward me, greeted him cheerfully with a loving smile: "Hi, bunny rabbit!" Solemnly he answered, "I'm not a bunny. I'm a boy!" As you accept each

child's personally described cloud picture, you help stretch children's capacity for creativity and ability to engage in pretend play, which is so important for all areas of learning.

Touching

At a petting zoo children can touch goats, sheep, llamas, and bunnies. At a nature park, state fair, or conservation center, some children may have stroked the pelt of a fox or a beaver. While picking up a gerbil from its cage, toddlers learn how to hold the animal gently under its tummy so that it is not squeezed or hurt. Gently, too, they stroke the velour softness of petals on a Japanese anemone bush. Cautious about thorns, preschoolers touch the velvety texture of rose petals. What a delicious, sensuous sensation! Held in arms, infants reach to feel bumpy tree bark, tree leaves, and flower petals. Lying on tummies, they feel tickly grass with their fingers. Watch a toddler with wrinkled nose and intense concentration as he leans forward, almost toppling over, to gently pat violets in the spring.

Squish! Crunch! Splash! Some parts of our bodies experience with delight the sensations offered by nature. Cheeks feel the invigorating sting of a sharp wind and the soft caress of a summer breeze. Feet feel different textures as bare toes squish through mud, sand, or grass. One mom, as she washed off her 6-year-old with a hose, affectionately and laughingly called out that he was surely her "mud man"! On warm days, a hose is handy when children have been squishing mud through their bare toes. On cold days,

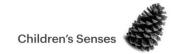

children tramp and crunch their boots through snow and exult in building and playing with snow. Invite children to talk about their experiences with different sensations on their feet or other body parts outdoors, perhaps from family adventure times or at school. Encourage sensory joys. In warm weather, messiness is a way for children to rejoice in the outdoors. They love to squish in puddles, dig in sand, and splash in water. Through these experiences they learn to trust the way their bodies work, observe natural phenomena (if you add water to dirt, it will turn to squishy mud), and love the outdoors.

Sandy, loamy, red, and black. As children dig and plant in the earth, they learn about soil texture. Some soil is sandy; other soil is crumbly, pebbly, or heavy clay. Try to obtain different soils from other regions for children to explore. In Georgia, iron mineral stains the earth a strong red color. Rich black earth makes possible the bountiful onion fields of central New York State. The salty Casa Grande soil, found in some parts of Arizona, supports desert life and grazing cattle. Some children may have helped their families add compost or loam to enrich the garden soil where they live. Older children can learn about the ancient Egyptians (and modern-day societies) who welcomed the annual flooding of rivers because flood-deposited nutrients provided fertilizer for their fields.

2 Nurture Children's Emotional Development

As children play, explore, and learn outdoors, using all their senses, nature arouses many emotions. One spring day in a classroom's garden, a child noticed the snouts of peonies pushing up through the earth. He ran to the rest of the group and yelled joyfully, "The red noses are up! The red noses are up!" His enthusiasm spread to the other children. A shy child with keen observation skills, such as this child, may be the first on a very early spring walk to spot tiny violet flowers; his discovery inspires peer admiration and helps him see himself as a contributor of knowledge. A child who has planted a seed and carefully nurtured it feels a rush of pride, awe, and joy as she watches the first petals thrust above the soil. In programs with outdoor planting space, children can grow their own salad greens, tomatoes, and green beans and feel pride in their industrious work to grow their food. Sweet potato plants, carrot tops, and the pits or seeds of avocado, grapefruit, and peaches can all be grown in pots in the classroom, even in the wintertime.

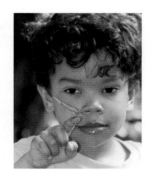

Connecting Children With Nature

While nature provides many delights for children, it can sometimes be scary. After a storm, encourage children to talk about how they feel when they hear thunder crashing or see flashes of lightning outside the window. Many chil-

dren confide that when they hear crashing thunder at night, they want to run into a parent's bedroom for comfort. Discussing their feelings give children a chance to share scary as well as positive emotions. Children feel comforted when they can safely express their worries to friends and trusted, nurturing teachers (Honig 2010).

Arouse curiosity about insects and spiders. Some children (and adults!) are wary of insects and other "creepy-crawlies." Organize a bug walk to help children become familiar with nature's creatures and what they do. Perhaps children will spy grasshoppers, butterflies, hummingbirds ("flying jewels"), moths, caterpillars, praying mantises, Japanese beetles, ladybugs with orange and black spots, centipedes, or spiders. Children who may initially be wary of even looking at a real bug may be fascinated by color photos of insects (Burris & Richards 2011). Talk about insects that are helpful to humans—such as bees and praying mantises, which pollinate fruits and vegetables or eat destructive insects—and about those that chew up crops or favorite garden plants, such as army bugs and Japanese beetles. When possible, watch honeybees dance as they teach other bees from their hive where to find delicious flowers, such as clover. Afterward, have children create a wiggly dance with their whole bodies and pretend they are bees showing their friends where to find flower treats in a meadow some distance away.

You might notice that overnight, a spider has spun a huge web between bushes, and there are glistening raindrops caught in the web. Just gaze for a while with children at this marvel of

construction. Encourage children to make up a poem or a chant about this elegant web. With older children, read *Charlotte's Web* by E.B. White aloud—again and again. They love this story in which Charlotte the spider is such a good friend to Wilbur the pig (Paley 2004).

Having found earthworms while digging outside, you and the children might decide to do a whole project about how helpful earthworms are in gardens. When a child digs in the earth and, with wide-eyed interest, holds up a wriggling earthworm, share her enthusiasm for this fascinating creature she has just unearthed. Earthworms are such helpful creatures, busy aerating soil and making the earth easier to prepare for planting and easier for tiny plants to push their fuzzy thin roots down into the soil. (Even young children will come to understand the meaning of sophisticated words like *aerating* if adults explain the words, demonstrate what they mean, and use them often in context.) While children do need to become aware of plants and creatures that can be harmful, such as poison ivy, poisonous snakes, or black widow spiders, let's support children's exploration and understanding of nature's creatures!

Use nature experiences to support cultural sensitivities. The vast number and varieties of creatures in nature provide a comfortable entry for teachers to talk about diversity among human families and cultures. Some monkeys are tiny creatures; some are large and muscular. There are slender, short gingko trees and towering giant sequoias. People, too, vary in size, whether shorter or taller, skinnier or broader. Differences make life inter-

esting! We should celebrate the variety found throughout nature—including among children and adults in schools and communities. Help children feel positive as well as curious in friendly ways about differences in skin color, abilities, or languages in the classroom. Read stories about friends in multicultural families, such as *Our Community Garden* (Barbara Pollak), in which a diverse group of friends play—and work—in their community garden.

Different fruits and vegetables are familiar to people from different cultures. Trying a variety of foods is one way to increase children's understanding of preferences and tastes enjoyed by other cultures. Invite families to share with the group dishes that are special to them, such as baba ghanoush, a delicious Middle Eastern eggplant dish. Mexican and South American families might introduce children to frijoles or tamales. Parents brought up in southern communities may be expert at making hush puppies and willing to share some of these treats with children. Jewish families might help the children knead dough for making braided challah bread. Children feel pride when their families' foods are enjoyed by others.

In addition to foods, invite families to share special skills with the children. A parent, in Native American tradition, might use sweetgrass to weave baskets that are beautiful, useful, and fragrant smelling (Kimmerer 2013). Watching a basket weaver enhances children's appreciation for the skill and care needed to weave the sweetgrass. Providing a variety of materials for children to try weaving, and other skills, themselves supports the development of children's fine motor and problem-solving skills.

Inspire children with stories about people who care for threatened animals. Read stories with children about endangered animals and the nature heroes who help them survive (remember to discuss what *endangered* means!). One example is *Turtle, Turtle,*

Watch Out! by April Pulley Sayre. Discuss the ways animals can be in trouble and how people help. Some sea turtles are threatened with extinction because of other animals—and also humans. Nature heroes arrange nets over turtle nesting sites on beaches to protect them and are present just when hatching occurs. They might protect nests with a barricade (black fabric fence) behind the nest to help direct hatchlings seaward. The Florida Fish and Wildlife Conservation Commission (Witherington & Martin 2010) suggests that helpers guiding turtles seaward on dark nights use flashlights with red filters, which don't seem to disturb the hatchlings (for more information visit http://myfwc.com/research/wildlife/sea-turtles/threats/artificial-lighting).

South American wild parrots, with their brilliant red and yellow plumage, are endangered in their forest nests. Nature heroes raise parrot chicks to adulthood, and then safely release the sociable, intelligent parrots back into the wild. In the Republic of the Congo, caring individuals (including one of my grandchildren) have nurtured orphaned infant chimpanzees. These helpers raise the babies, help them learn to forage for themselves, and later release the grown chimpanzees into the forest.

Awakening a passion for helping preserve wildlife often begins when an adult reads entrancing stories about the lives of animals in the ancient world as well as today. Many preschoolers enthusiastically learn about dinosaurs. National Geographic's *Little Kids First Big Book of Dinosaurs* (Catherine Hughes) offers 4- to 8-year-olds plenty of fascinating facts and stunning pictures of small, big, giant, and gigantic dinosaurs. Share *My Visit*

to the Dinosaurs, by Aliki, and *Prehistoric Actual Size,* by Steve Jenkins. For older readers, the whimsical book *Dinosaurology: The Search for a Lost World* (Raleigh Rimes) is full of flaps for children to peek under, with factual tidbits and fanciful details of the adventures of a fictitious explorer who reports finding live dinosaurs.

Many books include vivid and colorful illustrations that entrance young children as they learn about creatures and their environments. Scholastic Press publishes *Arctic Winter, Arctic Summer* (Susan Canizares & Daniel Moreton); *Polar Bears* (Susan Canizares & Daniel Moreton); *Counting Penguins* (Betsey Chessen & Pamela Chanko); and *Nests, Nests, Nests* (Susan Canizares & Mary Reid).

Children also enjoy books that emphasize kindness and cooperation among animals as well as more concrete concepts, such as color: *Ladybug's Lessons* (Sharon Streger); *Frog and Toad Are Friends* (Arnold Lobel); *The Puppy Who Wanted a Boy* (Jane Thayer); *Mouse Soup* (Arnold Lobel); and *Possum Magic* (Mem Fox).

Encourage children to share personal stories about plants and animals. Children who care for animals and plants often become good observers, aware of nature and of the need to care for nature's creatures. A kindergartner convinced his mother to let him keep his puppy near his bed on a mat by assuring her that he knew his puppy would not make noise at night

because he sang lullabies to the puppy—just like his mother had sung to him when he was younger. Perhaps a child's family adopted a pet from a shelter; ask the child to tell the story of how the family cared for that pet so lovingly that it gradually stopped acting afraid of them. Children may have plant stories too. They may feel protective of "their" plants that they have planted in the earth, watered, and cared for, like the 3-year-old in a Chinese preschool who explained to me, through an interpreter, that he was using a tablespoon to pile up earth patiently around his tomato plant. Heavy rains the night before had washed soil away from his plant and he needed to help it so it would not topple over.

Ask children to share their nature experiences. In upstate New York, after weeks of freezing temperatures and snow, one child reported that on a walk through the park on a recent weekend morning he and his dad had actually seen red robins. "And that means that spring is coming," he said joyously. Another child shared that she had noticed the flash of red on redwing blackbirds that returned after their long winter absence. During summer, some children told how they noticed little white butterflies flying right through the spaces in a fence; they could just fly anywhere without caring about fences at all. Another child told about seeing an owl poking its head out of a big hole high up in a tree during a walk in the woods with her grandfather. Yet another was delighted to share his story of a squirrel's entertaining antics on the family's apartment balcony. By sharing their nature discoveries with each other, children exhibit their growing recognition and appreciation of nature's amazing events, their storytelling skills, and their delight in the signs of each season.

Engage in hands-on nature projects. Bring nature alive for children through a class project in which they experience firsthand the daily lives of creatures. Start a butterfly nursery with caterpillars, watch them spin cocoons, and share children's awe when the caterpillars later emerge as butterflies (see Damien 2013). Children in the primary grades can graph the number of days it takes for metamorphosis—the process of caterpillar turning to butterfly—to occur (be sure to find out what time of year it is appropriate to release butterflies in your area). Read and talk about the handsome orange and black monarch butterflies in North America, which fly all the way south to Mexico each year to spend the winter in mountain forests that are more and more endangered by logging. If you live on the monarchs' migration route, perhaps children can participate in a tagging project (see www.monarchwatch. org). See "Bird Feeder Projects" on the next page for a hands-on project whose results will delight children and provide for some of nature's most vulnerable creatures.

Worms are great helpers for aerating soil as well as providing a tasty breakfast for robins. Children can help raise worms, if together you construct a worm bin where the children can practice taking care of the worms, adding peat to the bin, and becoming comfortable holding the worms and watching their development (see www.natureexplore.org/wormbin; also Bird 2010).

Bird Feeder Projects

Toddlers and older children alike will enjoy constructing a bird feeder and watching the birds eat from it. There are several types children can make, as well as others that can be purchased. For all bird feeders, the Cornell Lab of Ornithology advises hanging them either within 3 feet of a window or more than 30 feet away. This will help birds avoid crashing into your windows: From within 3 feet, birds leaving the feeder cannot gain enough momentum to injure themselves should they hit the window, and from a distance of 30 feet or more they are less likely to mistake the window for a way to get around the yard. Other tips to help keep birds safe can be found at *http://feederwatch. org/learn/feeding-birds/;* see also McLennan 2012.

Here are a few suggestions for homemade or purchased bird feeders. Search the Internet to find others.

- Roll pinecones in a mixture of birdseed, breadcrumbs, and vegetable shortening (or peanut butter if there are no children in the class with peanut allergies) and hang the feeders from a tree branch near a window. For more specific instructions, visit http://scdev.communityplaythings.com/resources/blog/2014/january/ feed-the-birds. You can also view a slideshow of the project unfolding with a group of toddlers at http://scdev. communityplaythings.com/resources/videos/bird-slideshow. Paper towel tubes can be used as a substitute for pinecones.

- String o-shaped cereal on string or yarn, tie up the ends to form a necklace, and hang from a tree branch.

- Decorate a clean, empty milk carton, cut a hole near the bottom, and fill with birdseed. Make a hole in the top to string some yarn through, then hang from a tree branch.

- Purchase a see-through bird feeder that can mount on a window. Although this does not give children a chance to help in the construction, they will enjoy seeing all the action in the feeder.

To help children identify the different types of birds they observe at the bird feeder, provide guides such as *About Birds,* by Cathryn Sill, or for older children, the National Wildlife Federation's *World of Birds: A Beginner's Guide,* by Kim Kurki. You can also use a website to learn more about the birds your class sees, such as www.allaboutbirds. org/guide/search. If you live in a cold climate, talk about how birds survive the winter and what they find to eat.

3 Plan Outdoor-Related Experiences to Enhance Cognitive Development

Careful observation and reasoning skills underlie much of children's learning. (Future scientists, in particular, need to constantly sharpen these skills!) Indoors, children group materials or pictured objects by one or more shared characteristics and learn cognitive concepts such as classification. Nature, too, abounds with opportunities for comparing and classifying.

Comparing and Classifying

Learning classification skills (grouping objects by one or more shared characteristics) and seriation skills (arranging objects in order of size or other characteristic) are important themes in the early childhood curriculum. Many teachers use form boards, geometric shapes, and other human-made materials to help children learn these concepts. But nature provides wonderful, sometimes subtle, opportunities to learn classification and seriation skills as children and teachers marvel at the ingenious differences among living creatures.

Shapes. Think of all the different shapes outdoors. Gingko leaves have a different shape than oak, maple, horse chestnut, hickory, or aspen leaves. Deciduous trees, which drop their leaves in winter, have leaves that look and

feel very different from the thin needles of evergreen pines or blue spruce. After collecting leaves on a walk, ask children what they notice that makes their leaves look different, such as size, number of tips, color, vein type, and texture.

Animals. Many children are genuinely interested in animals. Infants and toddlers love to explore picture books with mother and baby animals. Preschoolers and older children enjoy sharing stories about animals, particularly their pets, which might include kittens, parakeets, and even iguanas. Share nonfiction books about familiar and unfamiliar animals, like *Mommy Hugs* (Anne Gutman and Georg Hallensleben) *Underwater Dogs* (Kids' Edition; Seth Casteel), *I See a Kookaburra! Discovering Animal Habitats Around the World* (Steve Jenkins and Robin Page), *Meet the Howlers* (April Pulley Sayre), and *A House Is a House for Me* (Mary Ann Hoberman). Children will also enjoy many nature magazines featuring animals, such as *Ranger Rick Jr., National Geographic Little Kids, National Geographic Kids,* and *Click.*

Search the Internet for a colorful poster of dog breeds to share with children (for example, see the American Kennel Club's website, www.akc. org). Discuss the vast size differences in dogs, from the tiniest Teacup Yorkies to the largest Great Danes or Saint Bernards. Which dog is hairless? Which dog has the thickest fur? Why might a dog need a thick fur coat? Talk about how keen a dog's sense of smell is. Interesting questions spark causal thinking and reasoning skills, and offer an opportunity for older children to use reference materials to find the answers. You might also use a K-W-L chart, with columns for recording what children already **k**now about dogs, what else they **w**ant to know, and—after their research—what they **l**earned.

Children who live in rural areas may well be able to share the names of different breeds of cows, such as Holstein or brown Swiss, or of chickens, sheep, rabbits, guinea pigs, ducks, or geese. Research the different tasks that

horses are bred for. For example, racehorses are bred to run very fast; draft horses are used to plow fields and pull heavy loads.

Children who live in urban areas will see quite different creatures. Some children have a pet bird in a cage; others have a rabbit or a guinea pig in their apartment. They may be familiar with birds and squirrels and chipmunks outdoors. Flies come in through an open window, buzz around in a kitchen, and even walk on the ceiling. How do they do that? Encourage children to speculate and wonder about these visitors to their living spaces. Children will also see people walking their dogs or maybe even a pet pig on a leash. Some urban parks provide special places for dogs to play freely with one another. What can the children tell you about the romping that dogs enjoy with one another? Some children may want to act out in pantomime (and even add joyful barking sounds) the kinds of crouching, leaping, and friendly chasing that they have seen in a local dog space at the park.

Flowers. Like horses, cattle, and dogs, flowers are also bred for various characteristics. Tulips, impatiens, and others come in a vivid variety of colors; some thrive in shade and others in sun. Take children on a picture hunt for flowers. Use a camera, smartphone, or tablet to take pictures of the flowers that the children see. Back in the classroom, look at the photos of different flowers and ask the children the names of each plant. To further investigate flower names and characteristics, ask families to donate their garden catalogs of plants, trees, and flowers. Children can cut out the flower pictures to create a collage. Older

Pets: A Problem-Solving Opportunity

When children have experiences with pets, they not only learn about nurturing, they sometimes also develop amazing problem-solving skills. And it gives children a chance to offer advice and information to their special grown-ups! One afternoon Ilana, barely 3, sat up in bed after her nap and explained to her grandma that the dog had licked her face and ears and hair while she was just getting up from her nap. She told her grandma how to deal with such a problem: "Nana, if a person gets licked by a dog, and if a person doesn't like getting licked by a dog, they can just rub it off by rubbing their head on the pillow" (as she had just gently done). When her mom came into the room, Ilana said, "I just taught Nana if you get licked by a dog you can rub it off on the pillow."

children may want to arrange the photos in a certain order, such as according to their time of flowering (spring, summer, fall, and winter, if flowers bloom in winter in your geographic area), or by color or type, or by whether they are shade loving or require full sun. There are lots of opportunities for category learning and decision making.

Most children know some berry names: raspberries, strawberries, and blueberries. Blackberries, lingonberries, goji berries, elderberries, and loganberries are other varieties. If these berries, or others, grow in your area, provide some for the children to taste and compare. If not, look for them at a grocery store. Which are sweet? Which are bitter? Make a graph of what the children discover about the berries.

Measuring and Counting

The outdoors provides opportunities to enhance counting and other arithmetic skills. In late winter indoors, grow amaryllis bulbs. Every day children can use a clearly marked ruler to measure how fast those tall green leaves grow before the flowers appear.

Estimating and counting. Children love to gather bright yellow dandelion bouquets for their special adults. No matter how many dandelions a child plucks, more pop up again. Before children start to pluck the petals, ask them to *estimate* how many petals are on the dandelion. Making estimates fairly accurately is an important arithmetic skill that children will use throughout their lives, such as when they estimate how much their grocery purchases will cost.

Have children pair up. Give each pair two dandelions; each child counts how many petals he finds on each dandelion. If necessary, show children how to put a finger on each petal and slowly say just one number, in order,

for every single petal they peel off. This activity also enhances fine motor dexterity. Ask each pair of children to share how they counted. Did each dandelion have the same number of petals?

The rhythm of life. Noticing cycles of nature, children sense the orderly rhythms in the lives of plants and animals. Different creatures live varying lengths of time. The lifespan of a mayfly or a daylily blossom is just one day, but some California giant sequoia trees are centuries old, and some giant tortoises live more than 100 years. Have children compare the ages of their family pets, whether a cat, a dog, an angelfish, a guinea pig, or a parrot (which can live for 80 years!). Plant life spans, too, differ dramatically. Hydrangea, a perennial bush with flowers sometimes called snowballs, grows back year after year for decades. In contrast, annual flowers live one season and must be replanted each year. Biennials, like foxglove, bloom every second year after seeds are planted.

Discuss the seasonal changes with children. As they notice plants die and some trees shed their leaves in autumn, children begin to understand more about life cycles and earth renewal. Use these signs of decay and death in autumn as opportunities for discussion. Trees better withstand wintry blasts and the burden of heavy snow on boughs if they shed their leaves. Piles of fallen leaves raked up make a cozy cover for flowerbeds over the winter months.

Seriation. Nature walks become a springboard for categorization and *seriation*— the ordering of items in a sequence, such as lengths of string arranged from shortest to longest or cups ordered by the quantity of water they contain. Outdoors, what an assortment of objects children find to categorize and order: tiny pebbles, bigger stones, pinecones, acorns, leaves, small sticks, seed pods, scattered petals, and "maple keys" or "heli-

copters"—the seed leaves of maple trees that are secretly packed with baby food for a new tree. All of these items are great for counting, sorting, and making arrangements. You do not need vast expanses of grass or forest to do this activity; children who live in urban areas can find all sorts of treasures just by looking on the ground. Be sure to alert children to watch out and never touch poisonous plants such as three-leaved poison ivy with red on the stem. This attractive, low-growing pest trails over stone walls, but its oils on the skin cause outbreaks of miseries—itching red bumps all over, sometimes even into eyes!

Orderliness in time. Just as children learn seriation of items, they also learn orderly progressions *in time*. Plant blooming cycles provide a colorful means to teach this concept. A child knows that she was once a baby, is now a child, and will become a teen and then a grownup some day.

This makes it easier to understand the progression of blooming times for perennial plants. Depending on your location, tiny white snowdrops or crocuses or hellebores may appear first, poking through the snow. Of the spring flowering bulbs, which do the children notice come first: daffodils or tulips or irises? In the Southwest, aloes might be seen blooming in early spring. In northern states, some late-blooming flowers in autumn are chrysanthemums and giant red sedums. Each plant flowers in an orderly progression in time. Take pictures of plants blooming around your setting, starting in the spring and continuing through the growing season. Review the photos with children. Do they remember which flowers bloomed in the spring? What other clues in the photos help them identify the season?

Preoperational concepts. Preschoolers struggle with the Piagetian concept of *conservation*—the idea that an amount of something remains

constant regardless of configuration. It may look like a friend has a lot more birthday cake to eat on his plate, but he has cut his slice of cake into tiny morsels and has the same amount to eat. The treasures children gather from nature walks provide opportunities to enhance their understanding of conservation of number. Children first arrange their collected pebbles or other nature items in a circle on the table and count the total number. Then ask them to arrange the pebbles stretched out in a straight line, and then in a large triangle or a square shape. Each time, children put one finger on each item and count slowly. Surprise! No matter what shape children arrange the items in, the number is the same.

Preschoolers also struggle with conservation of volume, their strong perceptions overwhelming their ability to conserve quantity. If you pour juice from a large glass into many smaller glasses, some preschoolers decide that there is now more to drink because there are more glasses. But by reversing the procedure and pouring all the juice back into the original container, you illustrate for children that quantity is conserved. Likewise, a child whose cracker is broken into four pieces does not have more to eat than her peer who has one whole cracker.

Although most children will not fully understand conservation until they are past preschool age, teachers can provide many examples to help them begin to grasp the concept. Create a story (with pictures, or even little figures), for example, about horses munching on hay. When round or rectangular bales of hay are spread all over a field, young children might believe there is more hay than when the hay is compactly rolled into a bundle and stacked in a corner of the field, very close to each other. But in each case, the amount of grass in the field has not changed. Perceptions are strong for young children; adults need to guide them to use their thinking skills as well as their eyes as they struggle to understand problems of quantity or volume.

4 Encourage Children's Creativity With Natural Settings and Materials

Art projects based on nature deepen children's connection to the awesome richness of the outdoors and may help children notice details about nature when they are inside and outside. Watch birds at feeders in the yard or at windowsill feeders; watch gerbils or guinea pigs in their roomy cages in the classroom as they eat or drink or care for their young. Sometimes, looking outside the window, children notice that a rascally squirrel has somehow managed to leap to their bird feeder and is hogging all the birdseed. One day, children in one classroom looked outside and saw two bushy tails sticking straight up from their large, open wooden feeder. Cheeky squirrels were busy devouring a free birdseed buffet. The class decided that a different kind of bird feeder was needed so that little birds could enjoy the seed feasts. They all drew pictures of feeders and placements of feeders that might protect the birds' food from other creatures.

Outdoor Art Explorations

Children's experiences with nature and representations of it become a departure point for children's artistic creations with clay, playdough, crayons, and paint. Here are just a few examples of what children can do.

● Gather leaves, acorns, twigs, petals, dried berries, and pine needles on nature walks and create collages with them. (Make sure the items are not toxic.) Autumn leaves make colorful collages. When children cannot get outdoors in fierce weather, that is a time to make creative crafts and games with all the twigs, pinecones, and other materials that were collected outdoors in milder weather. Press leaves and other natural materials into clay to make designs. Monaghan (2007) provides dozens of such craft ideas.

● Collect sticks to draw with in sandy or damp soil. Children might victoriously scratch a huge letter, perhaps the first letter of their name, by using a stone or stick to trace the contours of the letter. They may carve spirals, circles, and other designs. With older children, examine photos of ancient Neolithic carvings of similar spirals and circles chiseled onto an ancient stone stele. Provide materials for children to make their own designs and experience a connection to those carvers of long ago. Add photos to the classroom of local wild places and animals to inspire children.

Imaginative Games

Nature inspires children who tend to be literal and who might benefit from more imaginative play experiences. Encourage them with imaginative games. Can children pretend to move like animals: leap like a kangaroo,

slither like a snake, gallop like a pony, creep along like a turtle, or thunder like a buffalo whose herd has just been startled into galloping flight?

Admire the imaginative games children themselves create, as an awed teacher shared in this description of the youngsters in her class:

> The kids pull their sand and water table out under a maple tree. One-half the class is in hiding on the other side of the yard. The rest are busily burying evidence in the sand. A 6-year-old informs me: "We're the native people. Our farms have been flooded and we're moving out. When we go we leave clues behind and then arty-arky—archeologists—find out about how we lived. I'm leaving some green cloth." "I'm hiding a chicken." "I brought a real arrowhead to hide!"
>
> Then it's time to flee. . . . The diggers get down to work unearthing rare finds and discussing their meaning. "Hmm, they liked to wear green." "And shoot chickens with arrows." "Was it Robin Hood?"
>
> Eventually the past and the present meet. . . . They troop inside for lunch, arms waving, ideas popping. "Hey, do we have books about the olden times?" ("Learning Happens" 2013)

Scenarios for Imaginative Play

Dramatic play can flourish in nature, which provides a wonderful setting for budding acting skills and plotting dramatic scenarios. For all children, but particu-

larly those who rarely play imaginatively, one teacher suggests using outdoor spaces for imaginative games. Tall grasses in a field offer hiding spaces for a child to crouch and pretend to watch for elephants stomping by or for monkeys to chatter and bark signals to each other as the troop jumps from

tree to tree. From a tree with a low, sturdy branch that children can reach without assistance, a child pretends to be a monkey swinging from the branch while the teacher stands ready to assist if needed. Take an imaginary safari with children to see giraffes and gazelles. Tie in book-reading times to outdoor activities to inspire children to engage in more elaborate creative play. Books about children from other times and many cultures can spark children's desires to incorporate aspects from the stories into their play.

The richness of natural materials outdoors inspires pretend play. Symbolic play is enriched when a child uses large, brown leaves from oaks or horse chestnut trees (buckeyes) to serve as "blankets" to cover the "babies"—plump little acorns with brown caps gathered from under the trees. Pinecones are plentiful in some wooded areas. One child gathered several fallen pinecones and asked for help as he struggled to push each one down into the ground. He told me these were his soldiers, and he was lining them up to lead them in a parade.

Acting out pretend mealtimes or playing restaurant becomes easy outdoors with sticks, nuts, seed pods, leaves, pebbles, and other materials found on the ground. Finding a four-leaf clover will take persistence and concentration (and maybe a bit of luck), but three-leaf clovers are abundant in many grassy areas, as are veronica (speedwell) and creeping Charlie. Their small leaves of different sizes and shapes can serve as different dishes, fancy foods, and special treats as children conjure up a meal or an outdoor ban-

quet. Leftover corn husks are pliant enough to fashion into corn-husk dolls to be invited to join a pretend outdoor picnic. Digging trenches in the dirt, children work hard to bury their "treasures" (outdoor items they have gathered) quickly so others can come and find them.

Seashore-Inspired Play

When the outdoor space includes sand (and water in warm weather), children can dig their toes into the wet sand and marvel at the patterns made by different foot pressures. If the sand is very wet, it is a wondrous material to create elaborate drip castles. Patience is required to squeeze droplets of glistening wet sand through the hands to create fantastic sand drip turrets and high castle arches. The endless possibilities for shoring up castle walls, creating dazzling new peaks, windows, bridges, and fanciful drip towers keep children playing happily.

Children build wet-sand mountains with curvy, sliding paths to allow a ball to roll around and around the mountain as it curls down from the top. Children can use bits of seashells to decorate their sand constructions, working with determination to create wonderful sand sculptures. "Children will develop problem-solving skills as they create tunnels and canals for their sand castles" (West & Cox 2001, 54).

One teacher set out on the floor a billowing blue sheet as a pretend body of water. He placed basins of sand at the edges of it, with seashells and plastic sea creatures hidden in the sand for the children to sift through and scoop out with their fingers. Afterward, children compared and excitedly talked about the treasures they had unearthed during their sand play.

Arrange other seashell explorations for children. Place seashell treasures in a wide, shallow, woven basket and set it on a shelf for children to examine. Support children's observation and language skills by asking them to describe the shells. If appropriate, suggest that children match a seashell in the basket with a picture in a book of seashell photos. The children will learn beautiful names like *olive shell, conch shell, scallop, oyster shell, pocket shell,* and perhaps even *chambered nautilus.* Children's artistic imagination is awakened as they admire the blushing pink colors on the interior of some shells and speckled outer adornments on others. One day I noticed several preschoolers huddled

near a basket of seashells, very absorbed in their activity. "Teacher," they exclaimed excitedly, "we're bakers!" With great pride, they rubbed the nacreous (iridescent) outer shells of large clamshells together, producing a steady stream of white flour-like particles.

In one class, kindergartners used large clamshells to create cultural montages. They fashioned fishers from pipe cleaners, stuck toothpicks into the pipe cleaners for fishing rods, and attached sewing thread to the toothpick rods for fishing lines. Then they seated each figure on the hinge of a clamshell as if the figure were fishing in the scooped hollow of the shell. Sometimes children's creative, artistic imagination leaves adults breathless with joy!

Scavenger Hunts

Outdoors, among large patches of tall grass, in bushes, and in tufts of plants, a teacher can hide a variety of interesting, nontoxic items and set up a scavenger hunt. This game challenges children and sharpens their thinking and memory skills as they problem solve with a peer where to find the hidden items outdoors. As children work together, they collaborate, practice negotiation skills, and share ideas about where to search and why. As they look for the

hidden items, they may notice interesting aspects of grassy tufts or how that tree root a few yards away is lifted well above ground level. Maybe a hidden item is just under that raised tree root! They use creative thinking to figure out the size of the hidden objects and pinpoint likely spots for this searching adventure. Reddy (2012) advises providing clues couched as simple riddles to whet the children's curiosity, such as "I can roll. Find me," (a ball) or "I am sticky. Find me," (tape) or "I can stand on you; but you can't stand on me. Find me!" (a floppy cloth doll; a soft leather pouch). Back in the classroom, children draw a map of where they looked outside. They draw the objects found and trace a crayon path of how they zigzagged back and forth while searching.

Before setting up a scavenger hunt, think about the children's developmental levels. Show younger children three-dimensional toys or items before hiding the items so they know what they are looking for. Hide only a few items for young children, as their sequential memory is more limited than older children's. For children who are easily able to imagine three-dimensional toys after seeing a large color photo, use pictures to alert them to the objects hidden. For children who want a further challenge, use small black-and-white photos. And for seasoned scavenger hunt players, use only words as clues.

5 Help Children Discover the Interconnectedness of Life

We are all connected—plants, animals, and people. We need similar things, such as food, fresh air, water, and exercise, to keep us healthy, and we depend on each other in different ways. When children experience the links between themselves and the world around them—through caring for pets, tending a garden, reading stories about nature and the environment—they begin to develop a passion for helping nature thrive. Even very small children begin to understand the *physical ways* in which we all need one another. When their empty tummies growl, infants need adults to read their distress signals and satisfy their hunger. Toddlers depend on adults to comfort them with a hug when they fall, feel scared, or scrape an elbow. Preschoolers who help feed the goldfish in their tank in the classroom know that the fish depend on them for a daily dose of fish food. Left in a flowerpot in the classroom over a long holiday weekend, flowers shrivel, their green leaves turn brown, and their stems droop. When the children return to school, they and their teacher talk about what they can do differently so the plants can thrive over the next long school holiday.

Children show compassion and concern for their classroom creatures as they discuss a good plan to keep the animals safe. The children talk about what might happen if they left the animals alone and untended over a lengthy break. They understand that animals can starve without food and water and that delicate, small animals will shiver with cold since the tem-

perature is turned down in the building to save fuel money during the winter break.

Many young children, because they have pets at home, will also understand that baby animals need loving care to thrive. Some have heard puppies whine with lonesomeness if shut out of a bedroom at night. Use familiar experiences such as these to illustrate how very important humans are in caring for earth's vulnerable creatures. Read books that show ways in which children are kind to animals, such as *Goose's Story* (Cari Best) and *Martha* (Gennady Spirin).

Benefits of Nature to People

Just as humans need to learn how to protect animals whose natural forest or grassland habitats are being destroyed, children can come to understand that many plants and animals act as natural protectors of the earth. Trees are wonderful natural protectors; their leaves produce oxygen that we need to breathe and live. To help children experience one way that nature is interconnected, plant flowers that attract birds and butterflies. A butterfly garden planted with specific bushes and plants (like a butterfly bush or coreopsis [tickseed]) attracts winged creatures. Bees and butterflies sip nectar and leave pollen behind as they hurry busily from flower to flower. Those other flowers then use that pollen to create seeds

Nature Inspires Observation

McLaughlin (2009) shared a conversation overheard between children that illustrates the power of nature to inspire children to become keen observers and explainers:

"That's an insect."

"No, it's not."

"Yes, it is. It has six legs. Let me count. One, two, three, four, five, six."

"What about those?" (pointing to the head)

"Those are feelers."

that grow into new plants. We owe much to those busy bees whose hard work makes it possible for plants to produce so many of the fruits and vegetables we love to eat and so many of the flowers that bring pleasure to our eyes and our spirits.

Bats, too, are natural protectors. During the day they sleep hanging upside down in trees, caves, and attics of houses. Each night they leave their homes to hunt for food, flying out in large swarms from the eaves of buildings, tunnels, and caves. Bats gobble up many insects that destroy farm crops. Talk with young children about how bats save plants as they eat up harmful crop-destroying insects.

Keeping a garden is a special way children can learn, from their own experience (planting, mulching, watering, and staking plants), how the world of nature works and how much each child can do to nurture living things. From keeping a garden, children reap benefits beyond food to eat and flowers to admire. Gardening requires work—digging in the ground (children love dirt!), planting, weeding, watering, nurturing, and finally harvesting. Through all these necessary activities, children come to realize the importance of work. They begin to realize the value of setting goals and following through on their plans in order to see their work come to fruition—literally. Their physical efforts give them a close connection to nature, to the particular plants they are tending. Children learn where their food comes from and what it takes to make sure it is healthy. While gardening, children become totally absorbed in their activities. Even children with shorter attention spans work with determination to dig deep holes, put in

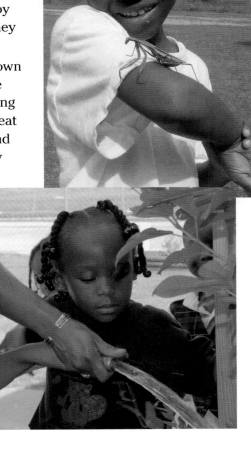

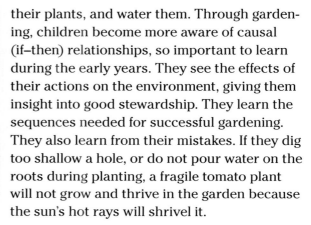

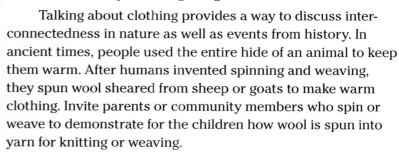

their plants, and water them. Through gardening, children become more aware of causal (if–then) relationships, so important to learn during the early years. They see the effects of their actions on the environment, giving them insight into good stewardship. They learn the sequences needed for successful gardening. They also learn from their mistakes. If they dig too shallow a hole, or do not pour water on the roots during planting, a fragile tomato plant will not grow and thrive in the garden because the sun's hot rays will shrivel it.

You might use children's gardening experiences as a jumping-off point for children to learn how food is commercially produced and how it gets to the markets in their community—and about all the people who work at the different tasks required for getting it there.

Talking about clothing provides a way to discuss interconnectedness in nature as well as events from history. In ancient times, people used the entire hide of an animal to keep them warm. After humans invented spinning and weaving, they spun wool sheared from sheep or goats to make warm clothing. Invite parents or community members who spin or weave to demonstrate for the children how wool is spun into yarn for knitting or weaving.

In ancient China, silkworms were raised and the silk fibers from their cocoons were carefully unwound so that skilled craftsmen could weave the fibers into silk fabric. Children may be curious about silk and other natural fibers for clothing, such as linen and cotton, which are grown from plants. If possible, provide samples of fibers for children to explore and compare. How are the fabrics similar? Which ones are smooth to touch? Which ones are rougher? Some plants provide dyes that give fabrics their vivid colors. Bring in some plants and berries (blueberries and walnuts are possibilities) that children can crush to create natural dyes and then test these dyes on fabric.

Awareness of Ecology

When children learn about the relationship of living things to each other and to their environment, they are learning about ecology. To explore ecology, start with where children are, literally: What animals and plants inhabit their community? their backyards? the fish tank in the classroom? How are those creatures able to live there? Animals and plants live in varied and specialized environments. Each creature has found a special way to live comfortably and safely in its space. Here are just a few examples to explore with children; some might be close at hand, others might be visited through a book and children's imaginations:

- If you turn over a rock, you might surprise a millipede that has settled there. What insects have the children in your program found living happily under a rock?

- Fish, of course, need water to live. In our center, toddlers sometimes took a goldfish "out for a walk" until we bought a heavy lid for the fish tank! What do children notice about the classroom animals? What do the animals eat? How do they sleep?

● Hermit crabs live in the empty shells of other sea creatures. A hermit crab finds an empty seashell and uses that as a new home as it scurries about in shallow waters, searching for food. Why do hermit crabs need a shell?

● Bears go into dens—which could be burrows, piles of brush, hollow trees, or rock crevices—and hibernate there all winter. Ask the children how they think this is possible.

● Some birds make nests in the hollows of trees, under the eaves of a building, or even—as some storks do—on chimney tops. Search online for sites that provide live video feed of active nests.

● Some flowers must have sunshine to thrive, but those on the floor of a forest need shade to flourish. Saguaro cacti lift their giant arms to the sky in arid deserts; water lilies thrive only in a pond or lake. Find and identify the plants that grow in your community.

● Mushrooms and other fungi grow in damp places. Children may find inky caps—edible mushrooms that sprout up in the grass after a wet season and turn to inky mush after

Helping People and Animals Find Ways to Live Together

There are real and varied challenges in today's world as civilization encroaches on wildlife territory and many animal species are declining sharply in number. Industrious beavers offer a good example, and make a great study project for older children. Beaver dams and ponds enrich wetlands with nutrients and actively help wetlands retain and slowly release water, increasing their capacity to act like sponges. This in turn makes flooding downstream less likely (Smith 2014). Yet how pesky those ponds sometimes seem to farmers whose fruit trees are awash in water. Helping beavers flourish while creatively finding ways to put pipes under beaver ponds to drain water from an orchard is one example of a challenge and solution—how people and animals need to find ways to live together.

a few days. They might notice how shelf mushrooms grow horizontally on an old, cut-down tree stump. Remind children not to eat mushrooms they find outdoors.

Exploring rocks. Rocks are the major material composing mountain ranges and cliffs. Rocks come in a seemingly infinite number of shapes, weights, and sizes and can be found almost everywhere on the earth and at the bottom of seas. Many children enjoy picking up rocks on a nature walk. Gather some different types of rocks for them to compare and wonder about as they explore samples with their hands and eyes. What subtle color differences do the children notice between rose granite and grey granite? Talk about how the mud and sands of ancient seas compressed over time to become sandstone rock and shale rock. As they hold hunks of layered shale rock, children may exclaim in surprise how easily those layers split apart. I once took some kindergarten children walking at the edge of a very shallow stream flowing from a distant waterfall. After I talked about the surprises that shale layers sometimes hide, the children spent hours fascinated with turning over shale rocks and wondering whether they could find fossilized leaves concealed between the layers. And some of them did!

How different white marble rock looks from smooth black obsidian (volcanic) rock. When held up to the light, rose quartz glows. With older children, use rock samples to talk about the difference between objects that are translucent and those that are transparent, which one can see through very clearly.

Rocks with the same name can have different chemical compositions. This is true for jades. Holding and examining hunks of varieties of the same rock minerals, children may be curious about what causes the differences in the rocks with the same name. Their early curiosity may in later years be further fueled by talks about different chemical compositions. In preschools and early elementary classrooms, some children, through hands-on experiences using a magnifying glass to examine particles of minerals in rocks, will feel the first stirrings of curiosity that will fuel their enthusiasm years later in a school chemistry or physics laboratory.

In Iceland, on the Hawaiian Islands, and in other lands, volcanoes spew glowing lava and hurl clouds of ash skyward. If children have heard about or seen volcanic eruptions from their reading, television, or other sources, they may have questions about eruptions. Red-hot lava soars skyward, slithers across roads and fields, and hardens into black rock across a landscape or falls, hissing, into the sea. Bring in some lava rocks so the children can feel them in their hands and talk about how light these rocks feel compared with heavier rocks. As you excitedly share the wondrous world of rock minerals with children, you may be planting the seeds for a child's lifelong delight in rock collecting and learning about rocks. After all, our own home, Earth, is an amazing hunk of rock in vast space—one that, fortunately, also has a generous atmosphere providing life-giving waters and oxygen to breathe and heavenly blue skies.

Learning about ecological disasters. Children may see and hear news stories about the powerful natural forces that impact people and the environment, sometimes irrevocably. Huge storm surges damage communities close to shore, even sending water pouring into subway tunnels in cities. Typhoons with winds of nearly 200 miles an hour devastate communities in the Pacific. Mountains are pushed up by the crashing of tectonic plates deep under our planet. Earthquakes are set off by one plate diving under another at a fault line. Towering tsunami waves sometimes follow after such quakes, destroying coastal communities. Older children who are aware of ecological catastrophes might decide to undertake environmental projects, such as raising funds for survivors of natural disasters. After watching television stories of houses swept away in east coast floods, some children in safe communities asked their families for sheets and blankets the children could bring to school and donate to those flood victims who had lost everything. Just as young children often dictate to an adult their stories, they can dictate words of sympathy and caring for other children who have lost belongings in environmental disasters and draw pictures to go with their messages. The center or school can then mail these compassionate messages to a school set up for the children who have lost their homes.

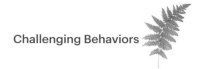

6 Use Nature Experiences to Help Children With Challenging Behaviors

Some children have difficulty with self-regulation. In the classroom, they find it hard to pay attention to a teacher or a task. They may wander from one activity to another with no real purpose or interfere with other children's activities. Struggling to control their impulses, they may have outbursts when they become even mildly frustrated. But outdoors, they can use all the bodily energy that is pent up in small classroom spaces by running, jumping, climbing, and twirling.

Outdoor Activities Help Improve Executive Functioning

Outdoor activities are one way to help children who have difficulty with executive functioning, or self-regulation, learn to master their own emotions and take pride in self-directed activities. Why are executive functions so important? They enable children to

- Take frustration in stride
- Set goals and work toward achieving them
- Think of all the steps needed to work on a specific problem or task
- Stick to a given task and concentrate on it; persevere to complete it
- Apply resilience to overcome adversities

● Accept responsibility for, and learn from, mistakes when necessary

● Switch gears successfully when frustrated or disappointed because a plan is disrupted or does not work out

Outdoor explorations can help children develop these important skills. Free to move their bodies in a larger, open space, children choose how to move—how far to jump or run or stretch or reach or roll on the ground. Space does not constrain them as it does in the classroom. When children have control over their choices in safe, interesting, and varied outdoor spaces where they can move freely about, they gradually come to feel that they can master their feelings or respond to frustration with less intensity. With a teacher's warm encouragement, they realize that they have choices for bodily actions, even when in the classroom. And if they tend to wander from one thing to another, they can let their attention wander occasionally outdoors; while daydreaming, they might hear rustling sounds in a tree or bush and spy a creature hidden there. Some children relate in a special way to butterflies who flit with such freedom from flower to flower; butterflies might feel like soul mates to those children who often restlessly move from one activity to another indoors.

Planning ahead is an important executive function skill. Occasionally, help children make a plan before beginning an outdoor adventure. Ask them to choose something special to look for or explore in a yard, park, or garden or on a forest walk. It might be looking for ants, grasshoppers, beetles, or other insects; spying dragonflies or flower buds; or turning over rocks to look for creatures. Having a personal choice of what to look for, and knowing that later they will share their discoveries with the group, helps children focus on their plans for the venture. They know and trust that once back in the classroom, each child will have a turn to describe to the others her self-chosen outdoor search activity.

Outdoor Activities Help Children With ADHD

Children with attention-deficit/hyperactivity disorder (ADHD) may have difficulty controlling their impulses and focusing their attention. Research shows that attention improves in children with ADHD who walk in outdoor settings with lots of greenery (Faber Taylor & Kuo 2009). Also, parents of children with ADHD report that their children are calmer after they spend time outdoors playing in natural spaces (Faber Taylor, Kuo, & Sullivan 2001). Encourage children who find it challenging to control their impulses or focus their attention to play large muscle games, such as jumping from one log to another or throwing a ball far and seeing how few *giant* strides the children can take in order to reach the ball again. Admire the effort it takes to hop on one leg from one tree to a tree quite a bit farther away. A highly active child may feel that her energetic movements are truly necessary to negotiate the large muscle activities the outdoors invites. Her strong need to be on the move is especially suited for outdoor games, such as Simon Says or follow the leader, or a playground obstacle course. Enhancing the self-esteem of a child who has perhaps been quieted and admonished indoors for her active behavior helps her feel happier and enables her to appreciate the importance of the outdoor world for her own well-being.

Outdoor Activities Help Children Who Are Tense

When children are anxious or tense they may have tight muscles and move rigidly. Some children have been sternly warned not to get dirty or messy. These children may need to learn to move with more relaxed muscles. Water, sand, and mud play can help the child whose muscles are rigid and the one who is too fearful to play or move freely. To encourage children to participate in these activities, keep a special supply of mud-day clothes available for warm weather. Then all children can delight in sliding down mud slopes, making mud pies, making mud footprints and hand-prints, and searching in a bucket of mud to find small toys a teacher has hidden. Building sand or mud castles with ornamental drips on top (see p. 39) is a soothing activity that helps a child unwind. Children may grin and relax while splashing and dancing in shallow mud puddles; they know this activity is encouraged and that at the end of the playtime the teacher will help children hose off the mud splatters and change into clean clothes.

Some adults feel uncomfortable themselves and may even squirm inside as they supervise children's play with mud or messy materials. Watching the joy on a child's face as she slowly, experimentally squishes muddy water through bare toes in warm weather or squeezes clay or playdough over and over into a shapeless mush, the teacher may recall her own long-ago wishes to explore materials freely. Empathy helps us relax about children's messy play.

Outdoor Activities Help Children Who Need to Let Off Steam

Children with pent-up emotions, perhaps because of home or other situations, may need safe outlets for their frustration. Help children find ways to safely let off steam outdoors—pounding on a log, kicking a ball, hurling a pinecone as far as possible. Trudging up a steep hillside on a nature walk is another way a child can work out frustration or strong emotions. He can whoop and yell loudly as he pounds the earth with his feet; he can lug heavy logs and twigs to build a fort. Balance these needs with helping all children revel in nature's awesome surprises and protect its creatures. Seeing a mother and baby squirrel or a bunny nibbling in the grass awakens compassion and tender feelings in young children; use such opportunities to help children learn how to treat creatures with tenderness.

Outdoor Activities Encourage Children to Play Cooperatively

Some children seem to always play alone or act in ways that disrupt other children's play. Some balk when asked to clean up or cooperate on a classroom task. But there is something magical about play-

Use Movement to Children's—and Your Own—Advantage

As I was carrying out an assessment with a preschooler, the child's mother, who had been warmly invited to stay, told me she had to run an errand. As she left the room she said, "Good luck. He never sits still." Grateful for this "tip," I asked the child to do me a favor by running back and forth in the classroom between every few assessment items so I could write down what he had just told me about the way he played each little game. He was so cooperative! Given the chance to move, he slid back down into his chair for another few items and was extremely friendly and interested in trying each task for nearly an hour. Time spent in large motor activities, particularly in nature settings, is a special gift for a child like this. Allowed to meet his need for frequent movement, he can more readily attend to other tasks. A little creative thinking can help you meet children's needs to move and explore—and meet your own needs as well!

Sing Outdoors

Take singing outdoors, where it can really soar! An active child can freely stomp and stamp out the rhythm of a song with her feet or bang it out with a short stick on a log or the playground surface. Invite families to sit with their children on the grass as you all belt out familiar songs together. As you participate with families in loud, cheerful outdoor singing times together, families may learn an appreciation of nature as a spacious green realm with limitless possibilities for enjoyment and learning.

When outdoor singing is not possible, use indoor singing times to encourage body swaying, hand clapping, and arm movements. This helps children enjoy the emotional release that singing, chanting, and actively moving can evoke. Even when young children have not mastered all the movements that go along with a particular song, they benefit from their own creative expression.

ing outdoors that inspires cooperation among children. Together they dig holes for posts to build a small twig house or fort. They loosen the earth and dig holes to plant flower and vegetable gardens. In wooded areas children gather stones to make *cairns*—stone piles that point the way on a path through the trees for other people so they won't get lost. This makes children feel special: They are helping people get safely through the woods. Many children have listened to stories in which people—often children, like themselves—have gotten lost in the woods, and their real-life efforts feel like helpful, important work!

Teachers in the West Indies report on the remarkable power of the outdoors to soften and engage children who show especially challenging behaviors:

> One of our goals is to provide regular connections with the natural world for primary school children while making school a friendly place. . . . Adult opposition came in the form of teachers, principals, and parents. However, our Earth Agent Day Adventures—a vacation day camp designed to train students to appreciate, love, and advocate for the Earth—showed us the priceless benefits of exposing children to nature. We facilitated the play of 27 children ages 6 to 9, most with extreme social and behavioral challenges, and everyone came out a winner. After allowing [our children] the

chance to run, jump, climb, build, and cook outdoors, we witnessed the magic of nature therapy.

This effort was coupled with our nationwide radio broadcast spreading a similar "get outside, hug a tree" message. One-third of our schools have reached the phase of creating a bio-friendly space and painting a mural. This phase allows us to use the community to facilitate learning by partnering with oil companies, parents, and neighborhood groups. Watching the interaction, hearing the language, and feeling the spirit of the group confirms for us that nature can heal. [The children] who participated are more independent, confident, polite, cooperative, and responsible now than at the start. (Constantine 2013, 96)

Outdoor Activities Help Children on the Autism Spectrum

Children with autism, like all children, can benefit from nature explorations, as Rosenow (2011) explains by sharing this story about the importance of learning to "listen" to what children have to say by observing their actions and the things they create:

[Sally] told of taking her young son "Chad" (who has been diagnosed with autism and language delays) and his two typically developing siblings to a nature-based public outdoor space. There, Chad discovered a large construction area where children could build with tree branches, tree cookies (cross-sections of tree trunks that show a tree's annual rings), and other natural items. Chad quickly became engaged in constructing a large rectangular structure. He used planks balanced on tree stumps to create places to sit, and he rolled four tree cookies up along the sides to look like wheels. Chad's siblings watched in amazement as their brother climbed into the structure and began to 'drive' (using another tree cookie as a steering wheel). "Mom," they shouted. "Chad made a car. Look at Chad's car!"

Sally talked with tears in her eyes about how amazing it was for Chad's brother and sister to see him in a whole new light, as a capable person with something important to "say." Sally [related] how that experience made her realize she must keep providing Chad with a way to "talk" to his family through visual-spatial material. (63)

7 Ignite Children's Interest in Nature With Media

The best way to interest children in nature is, of course, to provide plenty of opportunities for them to spend time in it! But don't overlook other activities that can supplement children's hands-on learning and exploration, such as books, websites, and videos.

- Provide books about nature to arouse children's curiosity and zest for learning about the world they inhabit. See the suggestions in the Resources on page 81.

- Look for websites with interesting creature news, such as "Ten Curious Facts About Octopuses" for older children (see www.smithsonianmag.com/science-nature/ten-curious-facts-about-octopuses-7625828/?noist). Also search YouTube for children's nature videos.

- Share reproductions of John Audubon's magnificent drawings of American birds and the superb flower drawings (often with an insect crawling on the flower) by Dutch artists a few centuries ago. Cathryn Sill's *About . . .* series offers books with beautiful drawings and simple introductions to a number of nature topics, including birds, mammals, marsupials, fish, rodents, and raptors, and a variety of habitats. *Maples in the Mist: Children's Poems From the Tang Dynasty* (Minfong Ho) combines poetry and lovely illustrations as the background for ancient Chinese poems, translated into English.

- Suggest that families set up a movie night to view movies about nature and the environment. Among the suggestions for young children provided by Common Sense Media are *Arctic Tale* and *March of the Penguins* (see www.commonsensemedia.org/lists/green-movies). Families might also investigate the television show *Wild Animal Baby Explorers,* for children ages 2 to 5, which combines animated characters and footage of actual wild animals. Children discover animal and nature facts, including science vocabulary. There is also the *Sesame Street Explores National Parks* video series, for children ages 3 to 5, in which park rangers team up with Sesame Street characters Elmo and Murray to visit national parks (see www.sesamestreet.org/parents/topicsandactivities/topics/nature). The videos emphasize exploration and inquiry and are accompanied by suggested activities for children. As National Park Service Director Jon Jarvis expressed, "We want to get kids thinking, 'Let's move, let's get outside, and learn something at the same time'" (Moore 2013, 1–2).

Share Fascinating Facts About Nature

Nature resources for children provide amazing facts that they enjoy learning, like the careful way a bower bird in Australia or New Guinea creates a shelter of twigs, clears the floor below of leaves, decorates the space with flowers, fruits, and berries, and then dances on that floor to attract a mate. Children are fascinated by things that are very small (ants) and things that are very large—like elephants. Younger children might like

to find out how much water an elephant swoops up in its trunk every day, or how much hay it eats each day, or why elephants use their trunks to toss dust and hay on their backs (often to get rid of itchy bugs).

For older children, pose some questions about elephants and then help children find the answers. How many muscles are in the trunk of an elephant, which is adept at picking up a peanut so daintily? (100,000 muscles) What was an early relative of an elephant? (*Moeritherium* [merr-uh-theer-ee-um], which was about two feet tall and had no trunk) How can you tell the difference between an African and an Asian Elephant? (African elephants are larger, about 10 feet tall and about 12,000 pounds.) African elephants' ears sort of resemble a map of Africa! They have a swayback and a rounded head without any bumps. Asian elephants (about 9 feet tall and about 10,000 pounds) have a smoother skin, and a high forehead with two bumps, and they have only one lip on the tip of the trunk instead of two.

Stimulate Children's Thinking Skills and Conservation Ideas

Challenge older children to work together to think of creative ways to solve a problem related to nature or the environment. In the "jigsaw technique," children with different abilities work together so that each child in a small group is responsible for one part of the topic. Children research their part, then put the pieces together for a final group presentation. Some possible problems for groups to tackle are 1) coal-burning effects on smog; 2) alternative energy sources; 3) effects of lake and river pollution; 4) effects on polar bears of melting polar ice sheets; and 5) the bleaching of coral reefs. Help groups identify appropriate resources to consult—books, websites, magazine articles, experts in the field, and so on. Children may decide to share some of their conservation ideas in a letter to the editor of a local newspaper. Further ideas can be found at alerts@aaas-science.org and bioactivist@biologicaldiversity.org. Also, contact the Union of Concerned Scientists at action@ucsusa.org.

8 Engage Families and Communities in Enjoying and Preserving Nature

Children engage in nature experiences not only in early childhood programs but also as part of their family and community lives. Find out what these experiences are. Invite children to share stories about their families' outdoor adventures, be it digging for worms in the backyard, growing pots of vegetables on a balcony, noticing weeds in the sidewalk cracks, or raising chickens. Support their experiences with activities in your program, and work together with families to further children's delight in and understanding of the outdoor world.

Ask Families to Share Their Own Nature-Related Experiences

All families have experiences to share. Some families have their own garden or participate in a community garden. Encourage children to bring in home-grown vegetables and share their gardening stories with the group. While shopping for groceries, parents can help their children learn how to tell when fruits and vegetables are fresh, and then admire how their children can pick out green peppers with smooth green skin and no brown spots or a mango that smells sweet and is slightly soft.

Ask families to share stories of children's enthusiasm for nature. One child spied a downy woodpecker with a vivid stripe on its back; one toddler in high rubber boots gleefully splashed each foot in a water puddle after a rainstorm. One child, feeling strong and helpful, victoriously gathered a heaping armful of twigs and sticks of different lengths to provide kindling for the family's outdoor barbeque. One parent recounted how she heard rustling outdoors and the children ran to the window to watch a wild turkey family walking in a stately fashion in their garden. Another family told about leaving the city where they live to go on a camping trip and the rich delight of all as they were surrounded by tiny fireflies lighting up the darkness. A child whose family lived in an apartment described the excitement of waking up one morning to see the potted geranium on the windowsill ablaze with red blossoms. One father talked about installing fluorescent lights on the ceiling over the family's windowsill, so African violet plants in pots could get enough light and produce pretty purple or pink flowers for the children to enjoy. Of course, some stories leave parents smiling ruefully. A mother described how her child's pet bunny escaped from its cage and left little clusters of rabbit pellets on the floor in several rooms.

Memories of special experiences with nature—whether indoors or out—stay with a child for a lifetime. When parents share their stories, everyone grows in rich awareness of the different ways children embrace a connection with nature. Remember to share with families their children's special nature experiences at school, too. Provide flyers with suggestions for parents to explore the outdoors with their children, such as going on nature scavenger hunts to find something wet or to find three flowers with different colors (Satterlee, Cormons, & Cormons 2014).

Encourage families to share their ideas for class and home activities for understanding the world around us and for helping to keep the earth a safe place to live and enjoy. At the dinner table, parents and children might share quirky nature and science news, such as the discovery of a gigantic octopus with 20-foot tentacles. Many creative solutions to pollution and conservation problems are in the news. To create synthetic rubber, scientists have tried using bacteria from rabbit feces together with steel smelting waste gases—an extraordinary innovation (Gelling 2013). From the silky secretions of slug slimes, scientists have created a sticky, viscous medical glue that may be able to replace stitches and staples in surgery (Williams 2014).

Support Family and Community Conservation Efforts

Weave conservation ideas and practices into the fabric of children's daily lives. Talk about topics children relate to, perhaps a worrying topic a child has brought up at group time. Older children may have heard family members discussing the cost of gas for a car or the cost of gas or oil for heating homes. Ask children what they think families need money to buy. They may chime in that they need money for toys or ice cream. Then ask them to think of places where they have seen the grownups in their families paying money to buy something. They may mention grocery stores, gas stations, shoe stores, and drug stores. Talk about how cars need gas to run and confirm that gas to run a car costs a lot of money, and groceries to cook meals also cost money.

Encourage older children to think about their own living spaces and share what their families are already doing to be friendly to the earth, such as

composting food leftovers and grass clippings or collecting rainwater in barrels for watering plants when the season is dry. Turning off lights when leaving rooms is another way many families help conserve costly energy. Some children may point out that their families do not throw away plastic grocery bags but do reuse them to line wastebaskets and to wrap some foods so they will keep longer in the refrigerator. Others might note that their families use reusable cloth bags for groceries instead of plastic ones.

Older children can investigate different types of light bulbs, such as LED and compact fluorescent bulbs (CFLs), which are replacing less-efficient incandescent bulbs. LED bulbs last 10 years or more, use less energy than incandescent bulbs, and improve visibility. Although they cost more money than incandescent bulbs, both CFLs and LED lights last longer and save energy costs in the long run.

Recycling. Recycling encourages early conservation habits. Just as young children might help sort socks and match them into pairs, they can separate and sort out cardboard and paper items and help stuff them into the recycling bin. They enjoy vigorously squashing cardboard cartons so they fit into the bin. Children can share with the group their family recycling routines and what their families do to recycle usable materials. One boy told the class how hard his mom had to look to see the number in the triangle on the back of a plastic container in order to find out whether the number was 1 or 2 and if that container should be recycled.

In some communities, instead of seeking contributions from families and neighbors for school materials or projects, older children collect recy-

clables for their school recycling program. What other ways can children think of to help the earth stay clean and healthy?

Reducing food waste. Brainstorm with older children all the steps of producing food. These include the farmers' efforts; perhaps the use of fertilizers to grow and harvest the food; packaging; transporting the food to stores; putting the food on the shelves in stores; and selling the food. The money spent on these activities is wasted when people waste food. Children may decide to create a food rule to help avoid wasting food, such as "Serve yourself as much as you need on a plate; and then take another portion later if you are still hungry."

Water conservation. Raise children's awareness of water shortages and conservation by reading stories of how precious water is, especially to families living in drought-stricken conditions. With school-age children, talk about water tables and scarce water resources in deserts and other dry areas of the world. In some remote areas where water is scarce, children sometimes have to walk miles to find a well and then carry back a heavy container of water. (I once helped a 5-year-old child in Morocco, with her permission, carry one of two very heavy pails of water—her daily job—up many flights of steep hillside steps to her small home in an alleyway.) Study the water cycle so that children understand that even if water seems to be

plentiful where they live, it is still important to conserve where possible. Brainstorm ideas of how the class can reduce water waste, for example, by soaking paintbrushes first in a basin rather than under running water to loosen dried paint.

Tooth brushing is another topic involving water. When we brush our teeth, much water is often wasted. A child might suggest turning the faucet off while brushing until it is time to rinse out toothpaste. This saves 4 gallons of water per minute. Bring in an empty milk gallon bottle so the class can see how much a gallon of water is and how much water they could save. With older children, talk about ways to conserve water while taking a shower. Shorter showers reduce water use and wastefulness. Turning off the water while using shampoo and conditioner saves more than 50 gallons a week.

Other conservation topics. With primary-age students, widen the conservation topics you study. Children may be intrigued by a discussion of food expiration date labeling. Despite what most people think, these labels do not indicate whether a product has spoiled. "Use by" and "best before" are just suggestions determined by the manufacturer to indicate when food is at its peak quality. "Sell by" is the suggestion for when the grocery store should no longer sell the product. There are no uniform criteria for any of these terms. Because people sometimes misunderstand this issue, good foods are often tossed out (Frasz 2013). Making large quantities of food at one time, such as simmering a big pot of soup, that can last for several meals will save money on gas or electric bills because families do not need to heat the stove as often. Can children think of more ideas so that cooking and serving food are more in harmony with conserving earth's resources?

Waste from packaging is enormous. Even dental floss comes in fancy plastic packages. Scientists have proposed edible packaging as a possible future solution (Risch 2013), although there are several challenges.

When asked to share their ideas about how to help the earth, some children talk about the need to keep the ground free of litter and to conserve water. One preschooler said, "You have plants and you water them." Another child explained that his family soaks a pot with burnt-on frijole beans overnight so that the next morning his parents can clean the pot using far less water (Honig & Mennerich 2013). What other barriers—and solutions—to conservation can the children think of?

Community and system-wide efforts. Together, all stakeholders in children's lives can work to promote system-wide changes to protect the natural environment. Since 70 percent of ambient air pollution comes from diesel emissions, school systems (as in Omaha, Nebraska) might consider using propane-powered buses, which are cleaner burning than diesel buses and save on fuel and maintenance (More 2013). A child care center can install motion sensors to turn outdoor lights on and off at night instead of leaving lights on all night to protect the building. Newer buildings can be made energy efficient with practices such as "solar panel arrays, high-efficient windows, and a geothermal heat pump system" (Buckner 2013, 16).

Look for other ways to help children and the school protect the environment. Partner with individuals from the community or school system with skills in woodworking and machinery to assist children in building birdhouses, birdbaths, bird feeders, pens for small pets, and frames for raised beds to grow vegetables and flowers. The National Wildlife Federation helps

Create a Conservation Contest

Invite children to think up catchy sayings that emphasize protecting the earth and promote conservation. In the classroom, children enjoy using small chants, such as "Going out? Lights out!" when leaving the classroom. Another chant might be "Don't throw it away! Let's use it for play!" Older children can create musical raps or post catchy class slogans that focus on preserving green spaces, conserving energy, and cleaning up the environment. All of these ideas can remind and motivate children—and adults—about steps they can take to preserve our natural resources.

K–12 students and teachers establish school wildlife habitats (visit www.nwf.org/How-to-Help/Garden-for-Wildlife/Schoolyard-Habitats/Create.aspx). If you are looking for ways to recycle a Christmas tree, consider using it in the schoolyard as a shelter for birds (National Christmas Tree Association 2014).

Your school or program might consider installing green bins that hold compostable material. In a San Francisco school cafeteria, leftover food and empty milk cartons are turned into compost. Students use the compost for the school gardens and sell the rest to local farmers (More 2013). Organize a school-wide event focused on reducing, reusing, and recycling materials. Invite families to share ideas for environmentally friendly activities with children. Collect ideas to share with other families, such as one family's restoration of an old desk found at the curb; the restored desk became a special place for the child to do homework.

Plastic waste from water bottles presents a challenge for all age groups. Americans buy half a billion water bottles every week (Hoffman 2013). Bottled water is sometimes partly tap water, and plastic can leach chemicals into the water. A target for school fundraising efforts could be to provide students with stainless steel water bottles and reusable snack packs.

Conclusion

As children grow in their awareness of the world, their love of nature, and an understanding of ecological well-being, they may develop a strong desire to protect the environment. Teachers can build on these feelings by encouraging them to think of creative ways they and their friends and families, individually and collectively, can help keep the world a place safe for plants, animals, and people. Hands-on experiences increase feelings of connectivity, ignite a special passion for the earth's richness, and inspire an increased desire to find caring ways to conserve and protect earth's creatures. Play and learning outdoors help children avoid a nature-deficit disorder (Louv 2008). Each year, April 22 is designated Earth Day. Together, in daily personal interactions, teachers and families make it possible to enrich every day as an Earth Day for children.

References

Alderfer, J. 2013. *National Geographic Kids Bird Guide of North America: The Best Bird Book for Kids From National Geographic's Bird Experts*. Washington, DC: National Geographic Society.

Bird, J. 2010. "Worms to Beans." *Teaching Young Children* 3 (4): 24–26.

Buckner, J. 2013. "Deep Green by Design." *Berea College Magazine* 84 (1): 16–17. www.berea.edu/wp-content/uploads/2014/03/summerfall-2013-small.pdf.

Buczynski, B. 2013. "5 Awesome School Gardens Helping Kids Eat Healthy." Care2, November 13, www.care2.com/causes/5-awesome-school-gardens-helping-kids-eat-healthy.html.

Burris J., & W. Richards. 2011. *The Secret Lives of Backyard Bugs: Discover Amazing Butterflies, Moths, Spiders, Dragonflies, and Other Insects*. North Adams, MA: Storey.

Ceppi, G., & M. Zini, eds. 1998. *Children, Spaces, Relations: Metaproject for an Environment for Young Children*. Reggio Emilia, Italy: Reggio Children.

Constantine, K. 2013. "Reflection: Earth Agent Day Adventures." *Wonder: Newsletter of the Nature Action Collaborative for Children*. January/February: 96. http://ccie-media.s3.amazonaws.com/nacc/wonder-209.pdf.

Faber Taylor, A., & F.E. Kuo. 2009. "Children With Attention Deficits Concentrate Better After Walk in the Park." *Journal of Attention Disorders* 12 (5): 402–9.

Faber Taylor, A., F.E. Kuo, & W.C. Sullivan. 2001. "Coping With ADD: The Surprising Connection to Green Play Settings." *Environment and Behavior* 33 (1): 54–77.

Frasz, D. 2013. "Food Expiration Date Labels Trick People Into Wasting Food, Money, and Natural Resources." *Earth Island Journal,* September 19, www.earthisland.org/journal/index.php/elist/eListRead/expiration_date_labels_trick_people_into_waste/.

Gelling, C. 2013. "On the Rebound: Scientists Revive Search for New Rubber Sources." *Science News* 184 (4): 26–29.

Hoffman, P. 2013. "What Really Happens to the Plastic You Recycle?" Care2, October 2, www.care2.com/causes/what-really-happens-to-the-plastic-you-recycle.html.

Honig, A.S. 1982. *Playtime Learning Games for Young Children*. Syracuse, NY: Syracuse University Press.

Honig, A.S. 2001. "Language Flowering, Language Empowering: 20 Ways Parents and Teachers Can Assist Young Children." *Montessori Life* 13 (4): 31–35.

Honig, A.S. 2010. *Little Kids, Big Worries: Stress-Busting Tips for Early Childhood Classrooms.* Baltimore: Brookes.

Honig, A.S., & M. Mennerich. 2013. "What Does 'Go Green' Mean to Children?" *Early Child Development and Care* 183 (2): 171–84.

InsectLore. 2013. *Miraculous Metamorphosis Curriculum: Teacher's Guide and Student Worksheets, Pre-Kindergarten.* Shafter, CA: InsectLore.

Kimmerer, R.W. 2013. *Braiding Sweetgrass: Indigenous Wisdom, Scientific Knowledge and the Teachings of Plants.* Minneapolis, MN: Milkweed Editions.

"Learning Happens." 2013. *Connect* (blog), November 12, www.community playthings.com/resources/blog/2013/november/learning-happens.

Louv, R. 2008. *Last Child in the Woods: Saving Our Children From Nature-Deficit Disorder.* Updated and expanded ed. Chapel Hill, NC: Algonquin Books.

McLaughlin, G.B. 2009. "We Need More Sticks and Grass! We Need More Beauty!" Community Playthings. www.communityplaythings.com/resources/articles/2009/we-need-more-sticks-and-grass-we-need-more-beauty.

McLennan, D.P. 2012. "Classroom Bird Feeding: Giving Flight to the Imaginations of 4- and 5-Year-Olds." *Young Children* 67 (5): 90–93.

Monaghan, K. 2007. *Organic Crafts: 75 Earth-Friendly Art Activities.* Chicago, IL: Chicago Review Press.

Moore, F. 2013. "Sesame Workshop Project Urges Kids to Visit Parks." *San Jose Mercury News,* June 4, http://www.mercurynews.com/entertainment/ci_23383657/sesame.

More, T. 2013. "Schools Go Green: Homework, Lunch, Buses Get an Eco-Makeover." *A Universal Life* (blog), September 23, http://tammore.wordpress.com/2013/09/23/schools-go-green-homework-lunch-buses-get-an-eco-makeover/.

National Christmas Tree Association. 2014. "Real Christmas Trees Are Recyclable." Accessed June 24. www.realchristmastrees.org/dnn/allabouttrees/howtorecycle.aspx.

Nature Explore. 2011. *Growing With Nature: Supporting Whole-Child Learning in Outdoor Classrooms.* Lincoln, NE: Arbor Day Foundation and Dimensions Educational Research Foundation.

Paley, V.G. 2004. *A Child's Work: The Importance of Fantasy Play.* Chicago, IL: University of Chicago Press.

Piaget, J. 1952. *The Origins of Intelligence in Children.* New York: International Universities Press.

Reddy, L.A. 2012. *Group Play Interventions for Children: Strategies for Teaching Prosocial Skills.* Washington, DC: American Psychological Association.

Risch, S. 2013. "Progress and Challenges for Reinventing Food Packaging for Sustainability." Presentation at the National Meeting and Exposition of the American Chemical Society, September 10, Indianapolis, IN.

Rivkin, M.S., With D. Schein. 2014. *The Great Outdoors: Advocating for Natural Spaces for Young Children.* Rev. ed. Washington, DC: NAEYC.

Rosenow, N. 2011. "Children Are 'Speaking' to Us Through Their Construction Work: Are We 'Listening?'" *Exchange* 199: 63.

Satterlee, D., G. Cormons, & M. Cormons. 2014. "10 Ideas to Get You and Your Child Exploring Outdoors." NAEYC For Families. Accessed June 23. http://families.naeyc.org/learning-and-development/music-math-more/10-ideas-get-you-and-your-child-exploring-outdoors.

Smith, S.E. 2014. "Want to Stop Flooding? Reintroduce Beavers." Care2, February 14, www.care2.com/causes/want-to-stop-flooding-reintroduce-beavers.html.

West, S., & A. Cox. 2001. *Sand and Water Play: Simple Creative Activities for Young Children.* Beltsville, MD: Gryphon House.

Williams, S. 2014. "Slug Slime Has Inspired a New Medical Super Glue." Care2, January 14, www.care2.com/causes/slug-slime-has-inspired-a-new-medical-super-glue.html.

Witherington, B.E., & R.E. Martin. 2010. *Understanding, Assessing, and Resolving Light-Pollution Problems on Sea Turtle Nesting Beaches.* 3rd ed., rev. Florida Marine Research Institute Technical Report TR-2. St. Petersburg, FL: Florida Fish and Wildlife Conservation Commission. http://f50006a.eos-intl.net/ELIBSQL12_F50006A_Documents/Technical%20Report%20TR-2_R.pdf.

World Forum Foundation & Community Playthings. 2013. *The Wisdom of Nature: Out My Back Door.* Ulster Park, NY: Community Playthings.

Resources

Articles and Books for Adults

Bailie, P.E. 2010. "From the One-Hour Field Trip to a Nature Preschool Partnering With Environmental Organizations." *Young Children* 65 (4): 76–82.

Banning, W., & G. Sullivan. 2011. *Lens on Outdoor Learning.* St. Paul, MN: Redleaf Press.

Baumgartner, J.J., & T. Buchanan. 2010. "Supporting Each Child's Spirit." *Young Children* 65 (2): 90–95.

Boise, P. 2010. *Go Green Rating Scale for Early Childhood Settings.* St. Paul, MN: Redleaf Press.

Bucklin-Sporer, A., & R.K. Pringle. 2010. *How to Grow a School Garden.* Portland, OR: Timber Press.

"Choosing a Classroom Pet." 10X. 2008. *Teaching Young Children* 1 (2): 5.

Cornell, J. 1998. *Sharing Nature With Children: The Classic Parents' and Teachers' Nature Awareness Guidebook, 20th Anniversary Edition.* Nevada City, DAWN Publications.

Cross, A. 2012. *Nature Sparks: Connecting Children's Learning to the Natural World.* St. Paul, MN: Redleaf Press.

Galizio, C., J. Stoll, & P. Hutchins. 2008. "'We Need a Way to Get to the Other Side!' Exploring the Possibilities for Learning in Natural Spaces." *Young Children* 64 (5): 42–48.

Hachey, A.C., & D. Butler. 2012. "Creatures in the Classroom: Including Insects and Small Animals in Your Preschool Gardening Curriculum."*Young Children* 67 (2): 38–42.

Honig, A.S. 1982. *Playtime Learning Games for Young Children.* Syracuse, NY: Syracuse University Press.

Kirchen, D.J. 2011. "Making and Taking Virtual Field Trips in Pre-K and the Primary Grades." *Young Children* 66 (6): 22–26.

Louv, R. 2012. *The Nature Principle: Reconnecting With Life in a Virtual Age.* Chapel Hill, NC: Algonquin Books.

Meadan, H., & B. Jegatheesan. 2010. "Classroom Pets and Young Children: Supporting Early Development." *Young Children* 65 (3): 70–77.

Nature Explore. 2007. *Learning With Nature Idea Book: Creating Nurturing Outdoor Spaces for Children.* Lincoln, NE: Arbor Day Foundation and Dimensions Educational Research Foundation.

Nature Explore. 2011. *Growing With Nature: Supporting Whole-Child Learning in Outdoor Classrooms.* Lincoln, NE: Arbor Day Foundation and Dimensions Educational Research Foundation.

Nature Explore. 2012. *Keeping It Growing: Sustaining Your Outdoor Classroom.* Lincoln, NE: Arbor Day Foundation and Dimensions Educational Research Foundation.

Nelson, E.M. 2012. *Cultivating Outdoor Classrooms: Designing and Implementing Child-Centered Learning Environments.* St. Paul, MN: Redleaf Press.

Pancheri-Ambrose, B., & Tritschler-Scali, J. 2013. "Beyond Green: Developing Social and Environmental Awareness in Children." *Young Children* 68 (4): 54–61.

Pelo, A. 2013. *The Goodness of Rain: Developing an Ecological Identity in Young Children.* Redmond, WA: Exchange Press.

Redleaf, R. 2010. *Hey Kids! Out the Door, Let's Explore!* St. Paul, MN: Redleaf Press.

Remaklus, U. 2014. "Putting the Garden to Sleep: Understanding the Meaning of Nature." *Voices of Practitioners* 9 (1): 1–20. www.naeyc.org/files/naeyc/images/voices/3_Remaklus%20v9_1.pdf.

Rivkin, M.S., With D. Schein. *The Great Outdoors: Advocating for Natural Spaces for Young Children.* Rev. ed. Washington, DC: NAEYC.

Rosenow, N. 2012. *Heart-Centered Teaching Inspired by Nature: Using Nature's Wisdom to Bring More Joy and Effectiveness to Our Work With Children.* Lincoln, NE: Dimensions Educational Research Foundation.

Salmansohn, P., & S.W. Kress. 2003. *Saving Birds: Heroes Around the World.* Gardiner, ME: Tilbury House; New York: Audubon.

Scardina, J., & J. Flocken. 2012. *Wildlife Heroes: 40 Leading Conservationists and the Animals They Are Committed to Saving.* Philadelphia: Running Press.

Selly, P.B. 2012. *Early Childhood Activities for a Greener Earth.* St. Paul, MN: Redleaf Press.

Shillady, A., ed. 2011. *Spotlight on Young Children and Nature.* Washington, DC: NAEYC.

Sobel, D. 2012. "Look, Don't Touch: The Problem With Environmental Education." *Orion* 31 (4): 64–71.

Sayre, A.P. 2013. *Touch a Butterfly: Wildlife Gardening With Kids—Simple Ways to Attract Birds, Butterflies, Toads, and More to Your Garden.* Boston: Roost.

Stone, M., & Center for Ecoliteracy. 2009. *Smart by Nature: Schooling for Sustainability.* Heraldsburg, CA: Watershed Media.

White, J. 2012. *Making a Mud Kitchen.* Sheffield, UK: Muddyfaces. www.muddyfaces. co.uk/mud_kitchens.php.

White, J. 2014. *Playing and Learning Outdoors: Making Provision for High-Quality Experiences in the Outdoor Environment With Children 3–7.* 2nd ed. London: Routledge.

Wilson, R.A. 2012b. *Nature and Young Children: Encouraging Creative Play and Learning in Natural Environments.* 2nd ed. New York: Routledge.

Newsletters

e.Brief, weekly enewsletter of Earthjustice, whose slogan is "Because the Earth needs a good lawyer." www.earthjustice.org/newsletter

Endangered Earth Online, weekly enewsletter of the Center for Biological Diversity. www.biologicaldiversity.org/publications/earthonline

Wonder, the enewsletter of Nature Action Collaborative for Children. Inspires families to embrace children' daily connections with nature. www.worldforum foundation.org/working-groups/nature/newsletter/

Websites

Children and Nature Network. www.childrenandnature.org

Green Hearts Institute for Nature in Childhood. www.greenheartsinc.org

National Wildlife Federation. www.nwf.org/Kids/Educators.aspx

Natural Start Alliance. http://naturalstart.org/

Nature Explore. www.natureexplore.org

Project Learning Tree. www.plt.org

Other Materials

The *Florida Wildflowers and Butterflies* brochure illustrates wildflowers and all stages of butterfly transformations, from eggs to larvae to pupa to adult. The *Monarchs and Milkweeds* brochure discusses how to grow the milkweed plants so essential for Monarch butterflies to munch on. The brochures also provide tips for gardeners to grow native plants. Distributed by the Florida Museum of Natural History. www.flmnh.ufl.edu/wildflower/books.asp

Growing Up WILD: Exploring Nature With Young Children Ages 3–7 is a program that offers activities and experiences to build on children's natural curiosity and wonder about nature and to foster learning in all areas. www.projectwild.org/growingupwild.htm

The program *Inspiring Children's Spirit of Stewardship: A Toolkit for Early Childhood Programs* (www.worldforumfoundation.org/working-groups/nature/environmental-action-kit/) is designed to help teachers address environmental issues in a developmentally appropriate way. Teachers can also share the corresponding family program: *Inspiring Children's Spirit of Stewardship: A Toolkit for Families.* https://ccie-media.s3.amazonaws.com/natureactiontoolkits/Family_Toolkit_ENG.pdf

The *Toolkit for Schoolyard Habitat Program Development* provides a framework for improving school habitat programs. www.fws.gov/chesapeakebay/school/PDF/SchoolyardProgramToolkit.pdf

Books to Share With Children

Share stories with children that help them learn about the interconnectedness of people and nature and interest them in investigating nature's wonders. Here are just a few suggestions:

10 Things I Can Do to Help My World (2012), by Melanie Walsh. Preschool to school age.

About Birds: A Guide for Children (2013), by Cathryn Sill, illus. by John Sill. Preschool to school age.

Arctic Winter, Arctic Summer (1998), by Susan Canizares and Daniel Moreton. Preschool to school age.

Bringing the Rain to Kapiti Plain (1992), by Verna Aardema, illus. by Beatriz Vidal. Preschool to school age.

Charlotte's Web (1952), by E.B. White, illus. by Garth Williams. School age.

Compost Stew: An A to Z Recipe for the Earth (2010), by Mary McKenna Siddals, illus. by Ashley Wolff. Preschool to school age.

Counting Penguins (1998), by Betsey Chessen and Pamela Chanko. Preschool to school age.

The Day of the Dinosaur (1987), by Stan and Jan Berenstain, illus. by Michael Berenstain. Kindergarten to school age.

Frog and Toad Are Friends (1970), by Arnold Lobel. Kindergarten to school age.

Goose's Story (2002), by Cari Best, illus. by Holly Meade. Kindergarten to school age.

The Happy Owls (2013), by Celestino Piatti. Preschool to school age.

Hey Daddy! Animal Fathers and Their Babies (2002), by Mary Batten, illus. by Higgins Bond. Kindergarten to school age.

A House Is a House for Me (2007), by Mary Ann Hoberman, illus. by Betty Fraser. Preschool to school age.

I See a Kookaburra! Discovering Animal Habitats Around the World (2005), by Steve Jenkins and Robin Page. Kindergarten to school age.

In the Garden (2013), by Elizabeth Spurr, illus. by Manelle Oliphant. Toddler.

It's Earth Day (Little Critter) (2008), by Mercer Mayer. Preschool to school age.

It's Our Garden: From Seeds to Harvest in a School Garden (2013), by George Ancona. Kindergarten to school age.

Jack's Garden (2013), by Henry Cole. Preschool.

Jamberry (1983), by Bruce Degen. Preschool to school age.

Ladybug's Lesson (2008), by Sharon Streger, illus. by Richard Johnson. Toddler.

The Little Gardener (2012), by Jan Gerardi. Toddler.

Maples in the Mist: Children's Poems From the Tang Dynasty (1996), by Minfong Ho, illus. by Jean & Mou-sien Tseng. Kindergarten to school age.

Martha (2005), by Gennady Spirin. Preschool to school age.

Meet the Howlers (2010), by April Pulley Sayre, illus. by Woody Miller. Preschool to school age.

Mommy Hugs (2003), by Anne Gutman and Georg Hallensleben. Infant to toddler.

Mouse Soup (1977), by Arnold Lobel. Kindergarten to school age.

My Visit to the Dinosaurs (1985), by Aliki. Kindergarten to school age.

Nests, Nests, Nests (1998), by Susan Canizares and Mary Reid. Kindergarten to school age.

Night Rabbits (2007), by Lee Posey, illus. by Michael G. Montgomery. Preschool.

Once Upon a Memory (2013), by Nina Laden. Preschool to school age.

Our Community Garden (2004), by Barbara Pollak. Preschool to school age.

The Perfect Pet (2003), by Margie Palatini, illus. by Bruce Whatley. Preschool to school age.

Pet Show (1972), by Ezra Jack Keats. Kindergarten to school age.

Polar Bears (1998), by Susan Canizares and Daniel Moreton. Kindergarten to school age.

Possum Magic (1983), by Mem Fox, illus. by Julie Vivas. Kindergarten to school age.

Prehistoric Actual Size (2005), by Steve Jenkins. Kindergarten to school age.

The Puppy Who Wanted a Boy (2003), by Jane Thayer, illus. by Lisa McCue. Preschool to school age.

Real Live Monsters (1995), by Ellen Schecter, illus. by Donna Bragenitz. Preschool to school age.

Turtle, Turtle, Watch Out! (2010), by April Pulley Sayre, illus. by Annie Patterson. Kindergarten to school age.

Underwater Dogs: Kids' Edition (2013), by Seth Casteel. Preschool to school age.

What the Sea Saw (2006), by Stephanie St. Pierre, illus. by Beverly Doyle. Preschool.

For additional book ideas, see "Green Books for Kids," a list of books for toddlers to school-age children about topics ranging from helping animals to saving the earth from the effects of climate change: www.commonsense media.org/lists/green-books-for-kids.

About the Author

Alice Sterling Honig, PhD, is professor emerita of child development at Syracuse University, where for 36 years she directed the annual National Quality Infant/Toddler Caregiving Workshop. She received the university's highest honor, the Chancellor's Citation for Exceptional Academic Achievement.

Dr. Honig has published 600 articles and book chapters, more than two dozen books, and several cassettes and videos for parents and caregivers, including a video on nurturing early language. She served as Research in Review editor for NAEYC's peer-reviewed journal, *Young Children,* for six years and has lectured widely in the US and abroad.

As a licensed psychologist Dr. Honig helps children and families. She was program director of the Children's Center, a pioneer enrichment project serving infants and young children and their families in Syracuse. As a volunteer she led sessions for the Onondaga County Mental Health Association to help parents with difficult divorce and custody issues. In 2013 she presented the first Dr. Alice Honig award in China to a prominent Beijing pediatrician. In 2014 Dr. Bettye Caldwell endowed an undergraduate Falk College scholarship in Dr. Honig's name.

Acknowledgments

I would like to acknowledge my deep gratitude to those mentors and child development professionals, especially Dr. Bettye M. Caldwell, Dr. J. Ronald Lally, and Dean Bernice Wright, who over the years furthered my career and nourished my passion to enhance the lives of young children and their families and educators.

I also want to express my love and appreciation for my grown children, Larry, Madeleine, and Jonathan. They are deeply loved and served as teachers in awakening my sense of awe, responsibility, love, patience, and creativity—so needed as we cherish and teach children.